Charles Redd Monographs in Western History

No. 4

Leonard J. Arrington

Thomas G. Alexander

A Dependent Commonwealth: Utah's Economy from Statehood to the Great Depression

Edited and with an Introduction by Dean May

Charles Redd Monographs in Western History

Charles Redd Monographs in Western History

No. 4

Leonard J. Arrington
Thomas G. Alexander

A Dependent Commonwealth: Utah's Economy from Statehood to the Great Depression

Edited and with an Introduction by Dean May

The Charles Redd Monographs in Western History are made possible by a grant from Charles Redd. This grant served as the basis for the establishment of The Charles Redd Center for Western Studies at Brigham Young University.

PUBLISHED BY
BRIGHAM YOUNG UNIVERSITY PRESS
PROVO, UTAH 84602

ISBN: 0-8425-1013-3

Printed in the United States of America
Additional copies of the monograph or other numbers in this series may be purchased by writing to Brigham Young University, Marketing (University Press), 205 UPB, Provo, Utah 84602.
74 .85M 4623

Contents

About the Authors

Leonard J. Arrington is Lemuel H. Redd Professor of Western History and director of The Charles Redd Center for Western Studies at Brigham Young University. At the time his paper was prepared, Professor Arrington was a professor of economics at Utah State University. Thomas G. Alexander is professor of history and associate director of The Charles Redd Center for Western Studies at Brigham Young University. A graduate of Brigham Young and Brown universities, Dean May is senior historical associate with The Church of Jesus Christ of Latter-day Saints.

Introduction

Dean May

The passage from territorial status into statehood has often been hedged about with obstacles bearing no relationship to the capacity of the petitioning inhabitants for self-government. Regional rivalries in matters of economics and politics have been the most common considerations causing Congress to delay the admission of territories long since their meeting the minimal legal requirements. Only in Utah, however, have the obstacles to statehood been deeply and intimately connected with the religious and social practices of territorial inhabitants. It took half a century of petitioning and waiting before Congress finally approved statehood for Utah in 1896. The concession, once it came, was not granted without assurance that distinctive and unique aspects of the Mormon kingdom would be changed—that miscreant Utah would be thoroughly and finally "Americanized" in preparation for statehood.

Leonard Arrington's choice of 1896 as a year dividing economic as well as political stages in Utah's development seems entirely appropriate, for the required changes in religious, social, and political practices of Mormons were accompanied by parallel changes in the economic realm.

From 1869 to 1896 Utah had been characterized by an unusually sharp bifurcation of its population—each group pursuing its own social, economic, and political patterns largely independent of the other. The Mormons, partly out of respect for the advice of their leaders, partly out of inclination, kept close to what Arrington has called the "well-organized, relatively self-sufficient ecclesiastical commonwealth" which had been their ideal since 1847. Theirs was an economy "based upon irrigated agriculture, village industry, and occasional organized efforts to take advantage of fortuitous windfalls." This was one Utah.

The other was quite as apart from this one in its individualistic hell-for-leather scramble to extract the mineral riches from Utah's hills as was the Jacksonian entrepreneur from the idealized Jeffersonian yeoman farmer. Utah was dotted in the seventies, eighties, and nineties with small mining communities whose lines of intercourse were circuited away from the farming villages of Mormons by railroad lines taking ores directly to smelters and factories in the East and returning capital needed for further development. Socially and culturally the mining communities had little in common with the Mormons, and what economic ties developed between the two societies were maintained at a discreet distance.

After 1896, however, almost as if Utah's new status gave her Mormon citizens license to indulge in more typically American pursuits, the two economies began gradually to coalesce. Accompanying this change was a trend toward the commercialization of agriculture, a rapid growth of commercial and financial enterprises, and the acquisition of the various small mining enterprises by huge corporations readily commanding sources of capital and having major economic and political influence in the state. In short, Utah's economy itself became "Americanized," taking upon itself institutional forms, patterns of development, and relationships between sectors more like those of Rocky Mountain areas not settled by Mormons. Henceforth the exigencies and opportunities of geographical, climatic, and geological endowment would shape Utah's economy more than would devout obedience to plans prepared by a central authority. Furthermore, as Utah's economy became more specialized and fastened ties into the erratic world of national and international markets, stability was bartered for rapid expansion, autonomy for dependency.

The three path-breaking studies in this volume, one by Leonard J. Arrington—"The Commercialization of Utah's Economy: Trends and Developments from Statehood to

1910"–and two by Thomas G. Alexander–"The Burgeoning of Utah's Economy 1910-18" and "The Economic Consequences of the War: Utah and the Depression of the Early 1920s"–emphasize the precarious nature of Utah's economy in the period between 1896 and 1929. Particularly striking is the dependency of a sparsely populated region far from major trade and manufacturing centers, with an economic structure deviating from national norms in its unusually heavy reliance upon mining and livestock industries. Utahns had occasion to learn, early in the twentieth century, an economic lesson which nineteenth-century economists failed to emphasize in their tracts on the virtues of international free trade.

Certainly if nations concentrate upon the production of commodities which they are able to produce at relatively less cost than other nations, and if trade is free, an increased prosperity will redound to all. And it may further be true, as classical economists argued, that the resulting interdependency will give nations a strong incentive to make political decisions favoring peace among themselves.

Regrettably, however, there are degrees of interdependency. A Portugal which manufactures only wine might find herself more reliant upon Italian bottles than Italy is upon Portuguese wine. The Portuguese economy could be drastically affected by a decision Italy could make rather casually–to accept a French offer to exchange cheese for Italian bottles. With wine relatively more abundant than glass, Italians would be quite willing to pay a slightly higher price for a wine enhanced by a hearty slice of ripened Neufchatel. In the meantime Portuguese peasants are idled and poor, the landlord's grapes rotting in the fields. They had the misfortune of concentrating their energies upon the production of that which their resources permitted them to produce at the least relative cost–a misfortune because the world demand for their product was not great.

The example is, of course, in the manner of economists, absurdly simplified. But if we place Utah in the situation of Portugal, producing metals and foodstuffs for a nation which generally found these commodities abundant and available at less cost elsewhere (Utah lands must be irrigated; Utah copper must be refined from relatively low-grade ores; both foodstuffs and metals must be shipped far to major population centers), we have a largely accurate picture of the economic circumstances in which Utah found herself during the period under consideration. Once committed to joining the nation economically, Utahns had little choice but to devote their energies to exploiting the resources they had. If others could produce more of the same resources at lower cost, so much the worse for Utah.

Leonard J. Arrington's study treats the 1½ decades following statehood, from 1896 to 1910. It is a period characterized nationally by the achievement of McKinley prosperity—an economy recovering rapidly from the panic of 1893 thanks to gold, Republicanism, and a heightened demand for agricultural products stimulated by crop failures in much of the world. Prosperity was interrupted momentarily by the panic of 1907, but soon regained previous levels, moving strongly into the unprecedented growth stimulated by the First World War. It was an auspicious time for Utah to complete her integration into national economic patterns—one which made the price of statehood seem to have been well worth it.

Professor Arrington in this study subjects the structure of the economy of Utah during the period to exacting scrutiny, emphasizing especially those features in which the Utah economy differed substantially from the prevailing nationwide pattern. The high reliance of Utah upon stock raising, metal mining, and transportation industries emerges as a predominating characteristic throughout the period. Only at the end of the period does Utah show signs of a change in this pattern, as the percentages working in the food manufacturing industries (though not in agricultural production) and in the manufacture of nonferrous metal products begin to edge slightly ahead of the national percentage figures. In 1890 and again in 1910 Utah employed a greater percentage of its workers in financial and clerical pursuits and in building and construction than was the case nationwide. But despite these signs of change, the prevailing pattern throughout the period was of an economy which until 1890 relied heavily in its outside trade upon the marketing of metal ores and of livestock. The growth of the hydroelectric power and sugar beet industries toward the end of the period suggested future changes, but did not alter the prevailing pattern significantly.

The first of Thomas G. Alexander's two studies concentrates upon the eventful decade from 1910 to 1920. Certainly the world war was the great event of this period, dramatically altering political, economic, and social alignments throughout the West—one of the few undisputed watersheds in world history. The devastation in Europe created a dramatically heavy demand for American farm products, lifting agricultural areas into a rosy moment of prosperity. Utah profited greatly from the wartime demand in agriculture and mining as well as in an incipient manufacturing sector. The optimism thus engendered led to the founding of new industries and the expansion of cultivation into lands which even in Utah had hitherto been considered marginal. Indisputably, these were for Utah flush times.

Professor Alexander has prepared in this study a detailed view of the Utah economy moving into unprecedented prosperity, expanding rapidly in all directions. Utah for the first time began employing a greater percentage of the working force in agriculture generally than was the case in the nation as a whole, as much the result of a dramatic drop in the number employed in agriculture nationwide as of the increase in the percentage so employed in Utah. Manufacturing was making headway in Utah, especially in food processing and in the manufacture of nonferrous metal products, but changes in the overall structure of the economy were not dramatic.

In the final study of this volume, Professor Alexander concentrates upon the depression of 1920-21 and its effect upon Utah's economy—an effect which, more than in the nation as a whole, had repercussions lasting well into the 1920s. The unusual severity of the depression was, in Professor Alexander's view, a consequence of the prosperity of the wartime period. More accurately, the heavy demand during the war for precisely those products which Utah could best produce led to an overexpansion of agricultural, manufacturing, and mining facilities of marginal productive potential. When, with the end of the war, that demand was cut off, unemployment and depression of unusual severity and duration were the result.

While Utahns living during the decade from 1910 to 1920 no doubt saw the high prices for farm products and metal ores as unmitigated benefits, Professor Alexander, with the advantage of hindsight, has interpreted them otherwise. In these two studies his overriding concern is to explain why Utah did not, as did the Pacific Coast states, pass into an "urban-industrial economy" during the early part of the twentieth century. The failure to do so, in Professor Alexander's judgment, is primarily a consequence of misallocation of resources caused by a period of high demand. When that demand ceased, the infant manufacturing industries of Utah were mortally wounded. Not until the 1950s did they employ as large a proportion of the whole working force as they had in 1920.

The insight Professor Alexander gives into the course of Utah's economic development from 1910 to 1930 is rich in detail and challenging in interpretation. The wartime boom helped to reveal the marginal quality of Utah's potential as a manufacturing center. In manufacturing, agriculture, and mining, as Professor Alexander has argued, Utah has played the traditional role of an unskilled laborer—sought after during periods of high demand, but quickly dropped when demand slackens. It is the marginal quality of her resources which accentuates the propensity to boom and bust, as demand quickens or declines in sensitive response to international and national movements over which there is no local control.

Though the studies in this volume do not concentrate upon the postwar period, some general observations might help round out the picture. A dominant force in the postwar economy, as both professors Arrington and Alexander have pointed out, is the storage and distribution industry serving the United States military. Certainly the economic impact of the military, both in this and in chemical and electronics industries, has helped build and sustain the "urban-industrial" development Utah failed to achieve before the war. It is obvious, however, that with this situation, as with the wartime boom, Utah finds her prosperity resting heavily upon factors over which she has no control. As

Rhode Island and Massachusetts are ruefully discovering, defense establishments thought to be permanent can suddenly and ruthlessly be withdrawn, leaving local economies in desperate straits.

There are indications, however, that recent reductions of the mineral and agricultural reserves America has enjoyed will bring fundamental and lasting changes to the economy of Utah. The long-standing national economic pattern characterized by an industrial plant expanding and prospering upon an abundant supply of energy and natural resources seems about to undergo an abrupt reversal. Permanently high levels of demand for mineral and agricultural products may lift Utah out of the marginal limbo in which her economy has wallowed since the early pioneer agrarian isolation was ended. Secure markets for the products Utah can best produce may well lead to a degree of independence Utah has not seen since statehood.

A Dependent Commonwealth: Utah's Economy from Statehood to the Great Depression

1. The Commercialization of Utah's Economy: Trends and Developments from Statehood to 1910

Leonard J. Arrington

Introduction

The economic history of Utah may be divided into four periods. The first began with the arrival of the Mormon pioneers in 1847 and continued until the completion of the transcontinental railroad in 1869. It featured an isolated but well-organized, relatively self-sufficient ecclesiastical commonwealth based upon irrigated agriculture, village industry, and occasional organized efforts to take advantage of fortuitous windfalls. The second period, commencing with the joining-of-the-rails at Promontory and continuing until the achievement of statehood in 1896, was polarized around two economies, largely separate and disputatious. One of these was the nucleated Mormon commonwealth, with its passion for unity and organized endeavors and its spirit of independence and permanence. The other economy was comprised of several hundred jerry-built mining districts, populated almost exclusively by non-Mormons, essentially atomistic and speculative and dependent on eastern capital to finance the removal of rich surface ores for transshipment to areas which could fabricate them for industrial and domestic use. The third phase, beginning with statehood and continuing until the outbreak of World War II in Europe, witnessed the beginning of a population outflow, the commercialization of agriculture, the emergence of a "business" sector, the rise of the copper industry, and, above all, the gradual coalescence of two hostile economies into one. The fourth phase, beginning in 1939 and continuing until recent years, has underlined the importance of federal expenditures in promoting the state's development—in construction and reclamation, in missiles and electronics, in conservation and recreation, and in the storage and distribution of supplies for the military.

The period to be discussed in this paper—1896 to 1910—marks the opening of the third phase. The ecclesiastical commonwealth, characterized by the self-sufficient village, and the exploitative, individualistic economy of the early miners and traders gradually merged into a partially unified and specialized economy based on commercial agriculture, mining, and smelting. Emerging into prominence were such specialized farming enterprises as sheep and sugar beets; national industrial corporations, particularly in smelting; and a host of specialized smaller businesses, such as canneries and beet sugar factories, which produced for regional and national as well as for local markets. This period also witnessed the first of many federal reclamation projects in the state. These and other federal enterprises were to become increasingly important in the decades to come.

As contrasted with the "pioneer" period, economic leadership passed from the agricultural valleys and scattered mining districts to the industrial and business communities in Salt Lake City and Ogden. Whereas The Church of Jesus Christ of Latter-day Saints had been the predominant economic influence in the earlier period, the significant catalysts in promoting economic development in the first decade and a half after statehood were scientists, engineers, and "outside" capitalist entrepreneurs. Because of the mutual interdependence of farmers, miners, and businessmen in the newly unified economy, there was an increasing degree of cooperation among all members of the economic community. This was partly "natural" and partly purposeful. With respect to the Mormons, the First Presidency and Quorum of the Twelve Apostles sought to quiet any feeling among their brethren that it was improper for Mormon businessmen to cooperate with those not of their faith in improving the business systems of their communities by stating in 1898 that "under the present laws of the land" this was not only the proper thing to do, but also desirable.[1]

In a sense, 1896 was the great watershed of Utah economic history, as it was of Utah political history.[2] That the basic structural change in the economy occurred in the 1890s and early 1900s was the result of the conjuncture of three trends:

1. Agriculture had almost reached the limit of cultivation—that is, the limit of cultivation on lands which could be irrigated with diversion canals dug from existing streams and rivers. The further extension of cultivation was accomplished by mastery of the art of dry farming, by the construction of storage reservoirs, and by the construction of larger dams and long, expensive canals which cut through hillsides and watered lands distantly located from the streams that issued from the canyons. This agricultural problem was magnified by the exhaustion or "waterlogging" of some of the irrigated fields which had been farmed since the early days of settlement.

2. With regard to mining, the other staple on which the economy rested, the easily extracted surface ore bodies were all worked out. As one journalist expressed it, "the eyes of the mines had been picked out."[3] Further mining would depend upon expensive deep-shaft mining which would require large sums of capital.

3. The development of manufacturing in the Midwest, East, and Pacific Coast regions, together with the improvement of transportation and communication facilities, caused Utah's infant manufacturers to become marginal, then submarginal. They could not compete with lower-cost, more efficient firms selling on a nationwide basis.

The three primary adjustments which followed the conjuncture of these unfavorable trends (and the high birthrate) were as follows:

1. There was a substantial migration to such marginal areas as the Pahvant Valley in Millard County, the Uintah Basin, and Grand Valley in southeastern Utah. This was coupled with an even more substantial out-migration to the Grande Ronde Valley in eastern Oregon, to south-central and southeastern Idaho, to Star Valley and the Big Horn Basin in Wyoming, to northern and central Arizona and New Mexico, to southern California, to Sonora and Chihuahua in Mexico, and to southern Alberta in

Canada. Most of the migrants accomplished colonization by means of Church-organized companies. Those which were particularly active during the 1896-1910 period included the Mexican Colonization and Agricultural Company, the Iosepa Agricultural & Stock Company, the Alberta Land and Colonization Company, the Nevada Land & Livestock Company, the Big Horn Basin Colonization Company, and the Deseret and Salt Lake Agricultural and Manufacturing Canal Company.[4] None of the locations listed was attractive or sufficient to absorb those desiring land to farm. The high natural increase of population, in other words, was outrunning the supply of land. By 1899 Church officials had concluded that it was no longer advisable for converts to gather in Utah, even at their own expense. The significant in-migration of Mormon converts, which had existed since the formation of the Perpetual Emigration Fund in 1849, was thus brought to a close. The new immigrants were brought in from southeastern Europe and Japan, essentially for the purpose of mining.

2. In order to pay for the consumer and capital goods which Utahns desired and imported from other regions, entrepreneurs were forced to move into the production of goods and services which could be marketed in those regions. What comparative advantages did Utah have? She had a rich endowment of minerals and an abundance of grazing land; her irrigated farms could produce fruits and vegetables in profusion; her location astride the continent required extensive railroad services; and she possessed a few manufactures, such as woolens and smelting, which depended upon her store of minerals and extractable agricultural wealth.

3. As the state moved away from self-sufficiency to a commercial economy, a further structural change occurred since there was suddenly a necessity for new banking institutions, new retail outlets, and new service establishments. The old general store, which served the infrequent demand for "store goods," suddenly became inadequate; there was now a need for dry goods stores, shoe stores, jewelry stores, liquor stores, repair shops, and dozens of other enterprises located on the Main Street of Utah in 1910. The statistics on this are impressive. In

1890 Utah had fewer than five thousand persons employed in retail and wholesale trade. By 1910 this figure had risen to well over twelve thousand. Similarly, in finance and clerical occupations there had been fewer than one thousand employed in 1890. By 1910 this number was well in excess of seven thousand. In the field of the services, there had been fewer than nine thousand in 1890, and this had risen to more than nineteen thousand by 1910. Percentage-wise, all of these increases were far greater than the increase in population.

Each of these fundamental changes, it should be emphasized, was initiated atomistically, as men of capital and enterprise—Utahns and "outsiders"—shifted their attention away from service to the local market and became interested in service to the national market. Once opportunities such as the mining of copper were grasped, the favorable cost-price situation tended to pull local labor and capital out of activities engaged in serving the local market and into the production of items such as copper which were in demand in eastern markets. These adjustments, in turn, attracted an inflow of capital, immigrant labor, machinery, and other goods from outside the state, thus providing the wherewithal of economic growth. Increasingly, the health of the economy came to depend on the continuance of favorable prices for the new staple exports. The most important of these, copper, suffered from an unstable price and uncertain technology, insuring that the state's economy would be subject to extreme fluctuations. It is also significant that much of the income earned from mineral exports was spent for Victorian homes along South Temple Street; for mansions, yachts, and vacations in the East; for political campaigns and propaganda; and, in general, for purposes that made no contribution toward the ultimate industrial development of Utah. Nevertheless, the earnings of farmers, ranchers, merchants, industrialists, and others made possible the purchasing power with which to buy automobiles, trucks, planters, harvesters, barns, corrals, and other equipment. (The value of farm implements and machinery in Utah rose from $1.2 million in 1890 to $4.5 million in 1910.) With farmers and miners buying more goods in the villages and towns, the business sectors in the villages and towns expanded. These expansions further increased the "residentiary" industries of the state. The rippling waves of income generated by a commercialized agriculture and an expanding mining sector accelerated economic change.

Population

According to the census, the population of Utah in 1890 was 210,779 persons. (The population at the time of statehood in 1896 is estimated at 250,827.) This rose to 276,749 in 1900 and to 373,351 in 1910. The growth in population from 1890 to 1910 was 77 percent, which was well above the 46 percent rate of growth nationally. This increase meant that Utah's economy would have to expand even more rapidly in order to provide employment for an increasing number of persons and also to permit a rising per capita income. Growth in Utah was particularly rapid from 1890 to 1900 in Box Elder, Juab, Tooele, Utah, and Salt Lake counties and in the counties of eastern Utah—Uintah, Grand, and San Juan. From 1900 to 1910 the growth was most rapid in the urbanizing regions of the state—Salt Lake, Weber, Davis, and Cache counties. Over the entire period, rates of growth of more than 100 percent were experienced in Carbon, Salt Lake, Tooele, Uintah, and Wasatch counties.

Utah's work force in 1890 consisted of 66,901 persons, or 32 percent of the total population. By 1900 the work force had risen to 84,604 persons, and by 1910 it stood at 131,540, which was 35 percent of the population in that year. As with the population, the work force rose more rapidly than the national average.

There is no way to calculate with precision either the total or the per capita income of Utah during this period of early statehood. Accurate income estimates by states are not available for the years before 1929. Using the statistical tools available, however, Richard Easterlin has made estimates of state incomes for the years 1880, 1900, and 1919-21. These enable us to make suggestive comparisons. Table 1.1 compares Utah with the United States as a whole, which, of course, includes the indus-

TABLE 1.1
Estimates of Income in Utah and the USA: 1880, 1900, 1919-21

	Contemporary Dollars			1964 Dollars		
	1880	1900	1919-21	1880	1900	1919-21
1. Personal income per capita, Utah	134	183	556	483	776	1,023
Personal income per capita, USA	175	203	658	630	861	1,211
2. Service income per capita, Utah	122	161	480	439	683	883
Service income per capita, USA	148	170	533	533	721	981
3. Service income per worker, Utah	438	526	1,443	1,577	2,230	2,656
Service income per worker, USA	426	444	1,356	1,534	1,883	2,495
4. Agricultural service income per worker, Utah	167	285	1,228	601	1,208	2,260
Agricultural service income per worker, USA	228	229	883	821	971	1,625
5. Nonagricultural service income per worker, Utah	658	680	1,529	2,369	2,883	2,813
Nonagricultural service income per worker, USA	622	584	1,520	2,239	2,476	2,797
6. Property income per capita, Utah	13	22	77	47	93	142
Property income per capita, USA	27	33	125	97	140	230

SOURCE: Simon Kuznets, Ann Ratner Miller, and Richard A. Easterlin, *Population Redistribution and Economic Growth, 1870-1950,* 2 vols. (Philadelphia, 1957-1960), 1:753-57; 2:185-87. I have converted the 1880 data into 1964 equivalents by multiplying 1880 figures by 360. Similarly, 1900 data were multiplied by 424, and 1919-21 data were multiplied by 184. This corrects to the price level effective January 1964.

trializing Northeast, the predominantly sharecropping agricultural society of the Southeast, the balanced economy of the Midwest, the Great Plains, and the Far West.

Two or three comments seem in order.[5] First, this data is consistent with some previous crude estimates arrived at by the writer on the basis of tithing receipts in one typical Utah region, Cache Valley. Whereas Easterlin estimates per capita incomes in Utah at $183 for 1900, average tithing receipts in Cache Valley for that year were $19.01, which would indicate an average income of $190 for that year.[6] Second, Utah incomes in 1900 were above those of the southern states, but below nearly all other states. They were well below income averages of all other mountain states except New Mexico. This low average was primarily because of the greater number of wives and children in Utah. Third, property income in Utah was only 67 percent of the United States average. This would seem to be typical of a pioneer society which had not yet accumulated very much by way of property or capital goods. This would be even more true of an equalitarian society such as Utah than of a society in which there were a few people of considerable wealth who could afford to accumulate property.

Just what did the persons employed in the state in 1890, 1900, and 1910 do for a living? The breakdown in table 1.2 shows the occupational and industrial structure of the state (and territory) for these years.

One way to secure an economic profile of Utah during the years specified is to compare the number of persons working in various occupations and industries with those in the United States as a whole. How many persons in Utah, relative to population, made their livings through the practice of agriculture, compared with the United States? Economists have a technique of making this comparison through what is called locational analysis. Lists of occupations and industries are drawn up, and the percentage employed in each occupation and industry in Utah can be compared with the percentage so employed in the United States as a whole. This is given in table 1.2. By dividing the percentage so engaged in Utah by the percentage engaged in that occupation in the United States, one obtains what might be

TABLE 1.2
Number and Percentage Employed in Each Occupation or Industry in Utah: 1890, 1900, 1910

Industry or Occupation	1890 No. in Utah	1890 Utah %	1890 USA %	1900 No. in Utah	1900 Utah %	1900 USA %	1910 No. in Utah	1910 Utah %	1910 USA %
All occupations and industries	66,901	100.0	100.0	84,604	100.0	100.0	131,540	100.0	100.0
1. Agriculture	20,031	29.9	37.2	29,247	34.6	35.3	37,241	28.3	32.5
a. General and crop agriculture	17,613	26.3	36.9	26,262	31.0	35.0	33,641	25.6	32.2
b. Stock raising	2,418	3.6	.3	2,985	3.5	.3	3,600	2.7	.3
2. Forestry and fisheries	347	.5	.7	214	.3	.6	176	.1	.6
3. Extraction of minerals	3,819	5.7	1.8	7,028	8.3	2.1	10,019	7.6	2.5
a. Coal mining	529	.8	.9	989	1.2	1.2	2,463	1.9	1.7
b. Metal mining	3,164	4.7	.6	5,951	7.0	.6	7,250	5.5	.5
c. Other mining and quarrying	126	.2	.2	88	.1	.2	306	.2	.3
4. Building trades and construction	5,538	8.3	5.3	4,009	4.7	4.4	15,442	11.7	8.0
5. Manufacturing	7,704	11.5	17.0	9,194	10.9	17.6	15,711	11.9	20.1
a. Apparel and other fabricated textiles	1,839	2.8	3.5	2,164	2.6	3.1	2,886	2.2	3.6
b. Clay, glass, and stone products	702	1.0	.8	314	.4	.6	1,089	.8	.8
c. Food and kindred products	876	1.3	1.3	947	1.1	1.1	1,557	1.2	1.0
d. Furniture, lumber, and wood products	327	.5	1.4	196	.2	1.2	294	.2	1.7
e. Iron and steel, machinery, and vehicles, including blacksmithing	1,601	2.4	3.4	1,738	2.1	3.1	4,891	3.7	5.8
f. Nonferrous metal enterprises	344	.5	.8	522	.6	.7	2,024	1.5	.8
g. Paper, printing, and publishing	463	.7	1.0	448	.5	.9	720	.5	.9
h. Shoes and leather products	783	1.2	1.4	643	.8	1.0	538	.4	2.2
i. Textile mill products	470	.7	2.2	451	.5	2.0	520	.4	2.2
j. Miscellaneous manufacturing	299	.4	1.3	1,771	2.1	3.7	1,192	.9	2.4
6. Transportation, communication and other public utilities	4,282	6.4	5.0	5,643	6.7	5.5	11,720	8.9	6.3
a. Railroads	2,094	3.1	2.1	3,414	4.0	2.3	8,199	6.2	3.5
b. Wagon and water transportation	1,958	2.9	2.6	1,927	2.3	2.8	2,449	1.7	2.2
c. Telephone, telegraph, and electric power	230	.3	.3	302	.4	.4	1,072	.8	.6
7. Wholesale and retail trade	4,825	7.2	7.2	4,871	5.8	6.2	12,246	9.3	8.9
8. Finance and clerical	1,929	2.9	2.4	3,613	4.3	4.8	7,141	5.4	5.1
9. Domestic and personal services	6,058	9.1	10.3	6,606	7.8	9.5	11,081	8.4	10.2
10. Professional and related services	2,608	3.9	3.9	4,427	5.2	4.2	7,971	6.1	4.4
a. Education	804	1.2	1.5	1,709	2.0	1.5	3,013	2.3	1.6
b. Other professional services	1,804	2.7	2.4	2,718	3.2	2.6	4,958	3.8	2.8
11. Public service	1,231	1.8	.8	898	1.0	.9	2,792	2.1	1.4
a. Military servicemen	785	1.2	.1	245	.3	.2	950	.7	.2
b. Federal officials and employees	446	.7	.7	165	.2	.1	571	.4	.3
c. State and local government[a]	......	.....	.....	488	.6	.6	1,271	1.0	.9
12. Unspecified and miscellaneous	8,529	12.8	8.4	8,854	10.5	9.0	....	.....	.....

SOURCE: The decennial census of occupation for 1890, 1900, and 1910. Also see Leonard J. Arrington, *The Changing Economic Structure of the Mountain West, 1850-1950,* Utah State University Monograph Series, vol. 10, no. 3 (Logan, June 1963), pp. 32-34, 43-45.

[a] Included with federal officials and employees in 1890.

TABLE 1.3
Economic Specialties of Utah: 1890, 1900, 1910

	Occupation or Industry	Number Employed	Specialty Quotient[a]
	1890		
	Employed in all industries	66,901	. . . . .
1.	Stock raising	2,418	11.65
2.	Military servicemen	785	8.36
3.	Metal mining	3,164	7.39
4.	Hunters, trappers, guides, scouts	33	5.00
5.	Chemists, assayers, metallurgists	49	3.50
6.	Builders and contractors	395	2.95
7.	Brick and tile makers and terra cotta workers	433	2.50
8.	Banking and finance	206	2.38
9.	Civil, mining, and other engineers	280	2.21
10.	Well borers	37	2.00
	1900		
	Employed in all industries	84,604	. . . . .
1.	Gold and silver mining	3,057	19.62
2.	Stock raising	2,985	12.17
3.	Handicraft textiles	88	10.00
4.	Mining engineers	75	9.00
5.	Copper, lead, and other mining	2,894	7.28
6.	Steam boilermakers	119	5.63
7.	Carpet manufacture	87	5.00
8.	Surveyors	55	3.50
9.	Hunters, trappers, guides, scouts	25	3.00
10.	Civil engineers	135	2.29
	1910		
	Employed in all industries	131,540	. . . . .
1.	Copper factories	1,576	24.00
2.	Gold and silver mining	3,167	15.75
3.	Copper mining	1,734	12.22
4.	Mining engineers	302	11.50
5.	Stock raising	3,600	9.13
6.	Forestry	104	7.18
7.	Beet sugar factories and refineries	190	7.00
8.	Lead and zinc mining	410	5.78
9.	Chemists, assayers, and metallurgists	199	3.75
10.	Military servicemen	950	3.60

called a "specialty quotient." The list of the ten leading economic specialties of Utah for the census years 1890, 1900, and 1910 is given in table 1.3 and reveals the unique aspects of Utah's economy during these years.

The development of these specialties, and of these to the exclusion of others, is, of course, partly a matter of geography, partly the consequence of unique historical circumstances, and partly the result of Utah's particular cultural configuration. Tables 1.2 and 1.3 reveal clearly the uniqueness of Utah's concentration on stock raising and mining during the years indicated. Utah also had, in 1890, far more than its proportionate number (eight times as many) of military servicemen, presaging a development which again became important during and after World War II. Utah also had during these years—and this is not evident in the tables—a relatively high percentage of dairymen and dairywomen, beekeepers, butter and cheese makers, lawyers, teachers, midwives, photographers, bankers and brokers, masons, blacksmiths, steam boilermakers, rug weavers, shoemakers, harness and saddle makers, dressmakers, builders and contractors, and U.S. government officials and employees. Although Utah had at each census more than its share of literary and scientific persons, there were fewer than a proportionate share of actors, artists, physicians, barbers, launderers, ser-

SOURCE FOR TABLE 1.3: The number employed is from the decennial censuses of occupations for the years 1890, 1900, and 1910.

[a] For every person engaged in these occupations or industries in the United States in relation to population, Utah had the number given in the specialty quotient column. To say this another way, the specialty quotient measures the number of people engaged in each occupation or industry in Utah, in relation to population, as were so engaged in the United States. Expressed mathematically, the percentages of the labor force employed in each occupation or industry in Utah and the United States were first determined, and the percentages so employed in Utah were divided by the percentage so employed in the United States. For example, for every person engaged in the business of stock raising in the United States in relation to population in 1890, Utah had 11.65 persons. Most economists refer to the specialty quotient as a location quotient.

TABLE 1.4
Leading Export-Base Industries in Utah: 1890, 1900, 1910

Occupation or Industry	Total No. Employed	% Producing for Export	No. Producing for Export
	1890		
Employed in all industries	66,901	.....	.....
1. Metal mining	3,164	86.47	2,736
2. Stock raising	2,418	91.42	2,211
3. Military servicemen	785	88.04	691
4. Steam railroads	2,094	31.97	669
5. Teamsters	1,568	30.56	479
6. Builders and contractors	395	66.10	261
7. Brick and tile makers and terra cotta workers	433	60.00	260
8. Blacksmiths	800	24.81	198
9. Civil, mining, and other engineers	280	54.75	153
10. Dressmakers	975	13.04	127
	1900		
Employed in all industries	86,604	.....	.....
1. Gold and silver mining	3,057	94.90	2,901
2. Stock raising	2,985	91.78	2,740
3. Copper, lead, and other mining	2,894	86.26	2,496
4. Steam railroads	3,414	42.20	1,441
5. Dressmakers	1,340	24.81	332
6. Blacksmiths	931	29.08	271
7. Military servicemen	245	48.19	118
8. Builders and contractors	275	39.39	108
	1910		
Employed in all industries	131,540	.....	.....
1. Steam railroads	8,199	44.13	3,618
2. Stock raising	3,600	89.05	3,206
3. Gold and silver mining	3,167	93.65	2,966
4. Copper mining	1,734	91.82	1,592
5. Copper factories	1,576	95.83	1,510
6. Military servicemen	950	72.22	686
7. Electricians and electrical engineers	904	47.92	433
8. Builders and building contractors	992	38.65	383
9. Lead and zinc mining	410	82.70	339
10. Civil engineers and surveyors	498	63.10	314

vants, policemen, bucksters, undertakers, paperhangers, plumbers, glassworkers, potters, bakers, lumbermen, cotton and woolen mill operatives, tobacco factory operatives, and makers of liquors and spiritous beverages.

The final item in our profile is the determination of the chief bases of support for the turn-of-the-century economy. This can be accomplished by means of "economic base analysis." In any society, certain industries are "basic," or town-building, and others are "nonbasic," or town-serving. Town-building industries include agriculture, which permits the people to satisfy their needs through direct production. They also include industries that produce a surplus which can be exported to other regions and exchanged for such items as the people cannot produce locally. The latter include mining, cattle grazing, and the manufacture of sugar. Town-serving industries, on the other hand, are those that arise to serve the needs of people attracted to the region because of the town-building industries. They include grocery stores, banks, repair shops, launderies, schools, and other businesses established to serve those residing in the region.

In addition to agriculture, which is always a basic industry, the principal basic industries are those which export surpluses outside the territory. A list of the leading export-base industries for the years 1890, 1900, and 1910 is given in table 1.4. Here are the industries which brought capital to Utah—which provided particular stimulus to economic development. Utah's overall dependence on exports for its livelihood was relatively

SOURCE FOR TABLE 1.4: The number employed is obtained from the decennial censuses of occupations for the years 1890, 1900, and 1910.

NOTE: The percentage producing for export is calculated as follows. First, the percentage engaged in each occupation or industry in Utah is divided by the percentage in that occupation or industry in the United States. The result is a location quotient. This list of location quotients is refined by excluding certain occupations and industries which are not export-base industries. The result is a list of export quotients. Each of these export quotients is reversed by dividing the export quotient into the export quotient minus 1.0. This technique is explained further in Arrington, *Changing Economic Structure.*

small—12.3 percent in 1890, 13.3 in 1900, and 13.4 percent in 1910. This demonstrates the lasting influence of the self-sufficient pioneer economy and the degree of diversification still existent. Throughout its history, Utah has been less dependent on a few exports than the neighboring states of Nevada, Idaho, Montana, Wyoming, and Arizona.[7]

Agriculture

Growth of sheep grazing. Despite the fact that agriculture did not expand relative to mining and manufacturing, there was real growth. The number of farms in Utah rose from 10,517 in 1890 to 21,676 in 1910. (Throughout the period, incidentally, more than 90 percent of Utah's farms were owned and operated by the farmers themselves—the highest ratio in the nation.) The growth in acreage in the 1890s was particularly spectacular—from 1.3 million acres in farms in 1890 to 4.2 million acres in 1900. This increase was largely in the amount of land placed under grazing. To be sure, the amount of improved land in farms almost doubled—from 548,000 acres in 1890 to 1,032,000 acres in 1900. But more than two million acres of land were being grazed in 1900 that were not being grazed in 1890. Since there was not a notable increase in the number of cattle, it is clear that this growth in grazing was largely for purposes of wool growing. The number of sheep in Utah rose from slightly more than one million animals in 1889 to almost four million animals in 1899. This coincides with an increase in wool shearings from less than five million pounds in 1889 to more than seventeen million pounds in 1899. Sheep were also the prime cause of the sharp rise in the value of farm livestock in Utah—from less than $10 million in 1890 to more than $21 million in 1900. This sharp increase in grazing in a state where vegetation was not plentiful or easily renewable led to many instances of overgrazing and was one of the considerations which led the Congress and president to set aside seven forest reserves in Utah, comprising some eight million acres of land. The Uintah and Fish Lake forests were set aside in the late 1890s; and the Manti-LaSal, Dixie, Wasatch, Ashley, and Cache national forests were set aside between 1900 and 1910. Henceforth, there were significant limitations on grazing, and the sheep industry declined.

Commercial crops. Aside from the extension of grazing, Utah agriculture began to specialize in the production of those products which were particularly suited to Utah soil and climate and to exchange these for outside products which could be imported more cheaply and efficiently than they could be produced at home. This growing commercialization in Utah agricultural production is evident from table 1.5, taken from the censuses of 1889, 1899, and 1909.

It is evident from table 1.5 that Utah agriculture was essentially diversified, with production revolving around the production of feed for livestock, food for the family, and an increasing volume of a few items (wheat, sugar beets, and fruits) for commercial sale. Much of the increase in production of specific crops, of course, was tied in with the increase in livestock grazing.

TABLE 1.5
Agricultural Production in Utah: 1889, 1899, 1909

	1889	1899	1909
Milk produced (gallons)	8,614,694	25,124,642	26,306,070
Oats and barley (bushels)	761,275	1,688,365	4,112,760
Wheat (bushels)	1,515,465	3,413,470	3,943,910
Irish potatoes (bushels)	519,497	1,483,570	2,409,093
Sugar beets (tons)	0	85,914	413,811
Hay (tons)	301,911	847,453	977,265
Apples (bushels)	56,633	189,882	350,023
Cherries (pounds)	554,680	1,198,512	6,914,712
Peaches (bushels)	69,910	85,315	143,237

SOURCE: Bureau of Economic and Business Research, University of Utah, *Measures of Economic Changes in Utah, 1847-1947* (Salt Lake City, 1947), pp. 49-50.

Agricultural items of interest during the 1896-1910 period are the following:

1. Most of the great beef cattle ranches of the 1870s, 1880s, and 1890s had died out or been drastically reduced by 1910. Marketing was handled increasingly by buyers who purchased shipments from smaller ranchers and farmers and sent the cattle out of the state to be fattened in the Corn Belt.

2. Utah, which still had five thousand oxen in the fields in 1890, had so fully disposed of them that they are not even listed in the census of 1900. In their place, of course, came "Old Dobbin." It is worthy of note that some of Utah's sturdy horses were sold to the British army for use in the Boer War.[8]

3. The poultry industry came slowly to Utah. As late as 1907, it was estimated that Utah raised less than 13 percent of the poultry consumed in the state.[9]

4. The thriving dairy industry of northern Utah was essentially launched in the 1890s and early 1900s, and the first evaporated milk plant, the Sego Milk Company plant, was established at Richmond in 1904. The first cow-testing association was organized in 1910 under the auspices of the Utah State Agricultural College Experiment Station.[10]

5. In 1897 the legislature established a State Bureau of Horticulture, which inaugurated a campaign to improve the quality and quantity of Utah fruit. Much of the credit for the development of Utah's famous fruit industry stems from the activity of this agency around the turn of the century.

6. The Deseret Agricultural and Manufacturing Society, which had assisted with the improvement of agriculture since its organization in 1856, came directly under the control of the new state government in 1896. In 1907 its name was changed to the Utah State Fair Association, and since that date it has sponsored the annual Utah State Fair.[11]

7. The most significant crop development was the launching of the beet sugar industry. This industry, which the pioneers had daringly attempted in the 1850s, was now, suddenly, the best-paying cash crop. Its success was due to the improvement in the chemistry of extracting sugar from the sugar beet, the Dingley and McKinley tariffs, and the desperation of Mormon

farmers, who were hard put to find a crop which could be exported for cash. That the farmers continued to produce crops during the first experimental years, even when the returns were negligible, is attributable to the Mormon Church's insistence, after the ill-fated efforts of the 1850s, on stressing beet growing as a religious duty. One of America's great economist-educators, Alvin Johnson, served as an economic expert for the Commissioner of Reclamation in the 1920s and had several things to say about sugar beet culture in the West. "No Nordics except Mormons," he wrote, "would have touched the beet for such compensation [$500 per family annual wage]. Mormon families took care of their own beets and prospered accordingly."[12]

Dry farming. Although efforts were made to reclaim more and more of the desert through irrigation, it was obvious that there would be many areas which could not be irrigated adequately. The practice of dry or arid farming—by which crops were induced to grow by utilizing the natural moisture in the soil and the rain—had been attempted as early as the 1860s, but without general success. A great interest was taken in arid farming during the early 1900s. A dry-farming station, established by a special act of the legislature in 1903, was set up in Nephi to determine the optimum conditions for dry farming.[13] As a result of this experiment and the wide publicity given to arid farming in general, it became one of the important methods of farming in Utah during the twentieth century.

Reclamation. The passage of the Newlands Act in 1902 expressed the interest of the federal government in reclamation, and federal funds were used to support surveyors, engineers, and agricultural economists to determine the most useful reclamation projects in the state. Several large and costly undertakings were contemplated, including a proposed dam and reservoir to make use of the resources of Utah Lake and of Bear Lake. These were rejected in favor of the Strawberry Valley project, which was begun in 1905 and completed successfully in 1922. The Strawberry Valley reservoir was the first federal reclamation project in Utah to be completed under the act of 1902. By means of a dam on the Strawberry River, a reservoir was created which covered six thousand acres and impounded

110,000 acre-feet of water. A three-mile tunnel—regarded at the time as a tremendous feat of engineering—led from the reservoir to Diamond Creek, from which it flowed via the Spanish Fork River into Utah Valley. The project made possible the irrigation of some sixty thousand acres of land in Utah Valley.[14]

Mining

Beginning in the 1880s, the small individual mines worked by transient prospectors were consolidated, one by one, into the great mining enterprises of Tintic, Mercur, Bingham, and Park City. These became focal points for railroads, smelters, and immigrant labor. Their influence occasioned the opening of the Salt Lake Mining Exchange in 1896, which did a brisk business in stocks during the next decade and a half. The number of shares exchanged increased yearly. The value of all minerals produced in Utah during the years 1890, 1900, and 1910 is given in table 1.6. The two mining districts which, perhaps, were most active during the period from 1896 to 1910 were Mercur and Bingham.

TABLE 1.6
Value of Minerals Produced in Utah: 1890, 1900, 1910

	1890	1900	1910
Gold	$ 680,000	$3,972,200	$ 4,032,085
Silver	8,400,000	5,745,912	5,652,164
Copper	157,035	3,046,885	16,204,828
Lead	3,071,880	4,227,872	5,426,284
Salt	126,100	151,662	185,869
Coal	552,390	1,447,750	4,224,556

SOURCE: *Measures of Economic Changes in Utah,* pp. 68-71. In addition, by 1910 Utah was producing $570,000 of Gilsonite. The total value of all mineral products of Utah by 1910 was just short of $40 million. From table 1.6 it is obvious that the most spectacular jump was in copper—the wonder metal of the turn of the century, which replaced silver as the chief Utah ore.

Mercur. The Mercur Lode had been discovered in 1879, with the gold discovery in 1883.[15] About 1890, John Dern (father of Governor George H. Dern) and others organized the Mercur Gold Mining and Milling Company and built a plant at Manning, three miles south of Mercur. When the group received news of the recently invented McArthur-Forrest cyanide process for the treatment of gold ores, they built a cyanide plant, the first built and operated in the United States. The plant was enlarged in 1893 to 100 tons, in 1896 to 200 tons, and later in 1896 to 350 tons.

The cyanide process, which required expensive equipment and high-voltage electricity, was designed for low-grade ore and enabled the extraction of one-half ounce of gold per ton in 1896. Construction of large mills, water pipelines, a thirty-two-mile high-voltage electricity transmission line, and a railroad to Mercur were among the investments which transformed the desolate canyon into productivity. A booming village was erected to house and service almost twenty-five hundred people.

A Dutch sea captain, Captain J. L. De La Mar, bought the Golden Gate group near Mercur in 1895 and erected the Golden Gate Mill. When this mill began operations in 1898, it became the principal employer in the district. In 1899 the De La Mar and Mercur interests united to form the Consolidated Mercur Gold Mines Company, which remained paramount in the life and activity of the town until 1917. The electricity on which the mill depended was provided by L. L. Nunn of Telluride fame, who built a dam across the Provo River and laid a forty-thousand-volt transmission line for a distance of thirty-two miles, his project receiving acclaim as the first long-distance high-voltage project in the world.

Although the gold extraction ratio per ton had declined below the profit margin shortly after 1910 and the mine had shut down, the total output of the Consolidated Company and its preceding component companies during the first decade and a half after statehood was more than four million tons, with a value of about $16 million. Dividends alone during this period exceeded $3 million.

Mercur is of particular significance because of the lift it gave to two prominent Utahns. The first was D. C. Jackling, who built the Golden Gate Mill and later moved to Bingham, where he pioneered the opencut method of mining copper. The second was George H. Dern, general manager and superintendent of the Consolidated Company, who later became governor of Utah and still later secretary of war in the cabinet of Franklin Roosevelt.

Bingham. While the rich surface ores of Bingham were discovered in 1848 and mined, milled, and refined in the early 1860s, the development of modern mining began in the period after statehood.[16] In 1896 Samuel Newhouse and Thomas Weir purchased the Highland Boy Mine and formed the Highland Boy Gold Mining Company to build a cyanide mill to process the gold ore which they planned to mine. A British company, Utah Consolidated Gold Mines, Ltd., was formed the same year with a value of about $1.5 million to provide the capital. As exploratory work took place, the miners discovered several ore channels carrying considerable quantities of copper. The company then decided to erect a copper smelter to reduce the ore. Commenced in 1898, this "modern copper smeltery" was completed and placed in operation in 1899 and was the first smelter erected in Utah primarily for the reduction of copper ores.

In that same year, a controlling interest in Utah Consolidated was sold by Newhouse and Weir to William Rockefeller and Henry H. Rogers—the Standard Oil crowd—for a reported $12 million. A new corporation, the Utah Consolidated Mining Company, was formed. Primarily because of the success of the Utah Consolidated venture, additional mining companies began to exploit the sulphide coppers of Bingham.

By the summer of 1904, the Salt Lake Valley was the home of three large copper smelters and a large lead smelter. However, the farmers living on lands adjacent to the smelters suffered extensive crop damage from the sulphur dioxide gas emitted from the smelter smokestacks, and after a series of farmers' meetings in the fall and winter of 1904-5, a suit was filed in the U.S. District Court of Utah. Eventually, a verdict was rendered against the four smelter companies which forced them to close their copper smelting plants in the Salt Lake Valley. This verdict heralded the end of Utah's sulphide copper mining and smelting boom. By 1907 all the smelters were closed with the exception of the lead smelter of the American Smelting & Refining Company, which paid "easements" to the local farmers and sufficiently controlled the release of noxious gas to secure the court's permission to remain.

In 1893 Newhouse and Weir purchased adjacent claims of copper at Bingham, sold interests to British stockholders, and formed the Boston Consolidated Copper and Gold Mining Co., Ltd. Much of the potential of these properties rested upon the huge quantities of low-grade ore. By 1900 the sulphide mine was almost on a paying basis, and the porphyry ore was being subjected to "elaborate tests." The company began to develop the disseminated porphyry ore deposits in 1905, commenced construction of a three-thousand-ton concentrator the same year at a cost of $1.5 million, and initiated steam shovels to strip the overburden from the mine in 1906. It was the first use of steam shovels for such a purpose. The panic of 1907 brought on serious problems of finance, and in 1910 the Boston Consolidated properties were absorbed by the Utah Copper Company.

Attention now shifted back to low-grade porphyry properties which Colonel Enos A. Wall had acquired at Bingham in 1887. Wall approached a number of mining "plungers" about these properties and finally interested Captain De La Mar, who sent several persons from his staff to investigate the properties. These investigations, coming in 1895 when the price of copper was declining, were discouraging, and De La Mar dropped his option. In 1898 De La Mar asked for a new option, sending Robert C. Gemmell and Daniel C. Jackling to do exploratory work and make sampling tests. Despite a favorable report from Jackling and Gemmell, De La Mar again dropped an option to buy all but a quarter interest.

In 1903 the enterprising Jackling, who could not forget the mountain of porphyry, was able to persuade his old Colorado friends Charles M. MacNeill and Spencer Penrose to purchase Wall's claims. The result was the organization of the Utah Copper Company. After successful experimentation with a small concentration mill working on underground ores, the group was able to enlist the financial support of the

Guggenheims and constructed a six-thousand-ton concentrating mill at Magna and a large smelter at Garfield. Upon the completion of these facilities in 1906—they represented the largest copper-reducing facilities in the world—Utah Copper initiated opencut mining operations at its Bingham porphyry mines. By 1907 the concentrator, the smelter, and the opencut mining, in which $8 million had been invested, were operating full-scale. By 1909 the equipment and facilities at the mine included 11 steam shovels, 21 locomotives, 145 stripping dump cars, and 16 miles of railroad trackage.

In 1910 Utah Copper combined with Boston Consolidated. Samuel Untermeyer, the New York lawyer who engineered the deal, received $581,250 in cash from Utah Copper, 3,250 of the 310,000 shares of Utah Copper stock (value about $62.50 per share), and an additional $193,750 from Boston Consolidated. The total fee is said to have been the largest ever paid a lawyer for such a deal. The merger set the stage for a prolonged period of growth and prosperity at the Utah Copper Mine.

Around 1910 John D. Rockefeller visited the facilities and viewed the beehive of activity created by the numerous steam shovels restlessly working to tear the green ore from two dozen terraces that lined the mountain from its base to its very top. Excitedly he exclaimed, "It's the greatest industrial sight in the world!" [17]

Coal. It appears evident that, at first, more interest was shown in the more spectacular metals than in coal. But the needs of railroads, the existence of railroads to exploit and market the fuel, and the skyrocketing demand for coal for smelting stimulated development of the industry. Despite increased output by the thirteen mines of the state, however, a coal shortage plagued Utah, and much was imported from Wyoming.[18]

Coal mining had its greatest boost when the Denver & Rio Grande Western Railroad opened up the vast deposits at Carbon County in 1882.[19] A subsidiary of D&RGW was the Utah Fuel Company, which owned the Scofield, Castle Gate, Sunnyside, and other properties and was the largest coal-mining firm in Utah during the 1896-1910 period. In the year 1900 Utah coal production, for the first time, topped one million tons, and in that year Utah Fuel mined 90 percent of Utah's coal. (In earlier decades, the Union Pacific Railroad Company had been Utah's chief coal supplier.) After 1906 a number of independent producers led by Charles N. Strevell of Independent Coal and Coke Company, Fred and Arthur Sweet of Standard Coal Company, and J. William Knight of Spring Canyon Coal Company sought to compete in the production and marketing of coal. In response to the challenge to its supremacy, Utah Fuel resorted to practices which many contemporary observers condemned.

The growth of coal mining in the years being treated occurred at a time when wages were low, health and safety hazards high, and union organization weak or nonexistent. In 1896 the state legislature sought to intervene by limiting the hours of work in the mines to eight and prohibiting the employment of children under fourteen. Many of the workers lived under unhealthful conditions in company towns. By 1909 immigrants made up more than half of the labor force, and Greeks, Finns, Austrians, Italians, Japanese, and others often had to set up tents or shacks in the dirt, without sewage or water facilities. Labor agents, gamblers, and labor agitators preyed upon these immigrant miners.[20] Since most of the coal was mined by hand or shot off the solid, accidents were frequent. During the Scofield explosion of May 1, 1900, two hundred men were killed. A major disturbance occurred during the winter of 1903-4, when the United Mine Workers tried to organize the miners and demanded a raise in wages from $2.50 to $3.50 per day and abolition of the company scrip system. Governor Heber M. Wells called out the National Guard in November, and a number of "young Mormons" broke the strike, causing the striking miners to lose their jobs.

Uranium. Two significant events occurred in 1898 which were to affect Utah profoundly. The first was the isolation of radium from uranium pitchblende by Pierre and Marie Curie. The second was the identification—by a French mining engineer, Charles Poulot—of a bright yellow substance found in the Colorado Plateau region as carnotite.[21] There resulted a demand for pitchblende for experimental and other purposes, most of the substance being shipped to Germany and France. By 1906 an estimated two hundred tons of ore were mined annually in Colorado and Utah. The mining of carnotite and pitchblende remained a minor industry but presaged the major emphasis of later days.

Oil and gas. A great interest was shown in iron and oil in Utah during these years. A number of mining concerns had hopes of making Utah the site of a large iron industry—a hope which finally bore fruit in 1922 and, even more so, during World War II. It was also hoped that it would be possible to develop oil fields into a profitable venture. The oil which was discovered seemed at first to be of high quality and to be present in large quantities in lands extending from Rich County on the north to the San Juan on the south.[22] Several oil and gas wells were drilled in various parts of the state in the years after statehood, particularly from 1906 to 1910.[23] In 1907 the Virgin River Oil Company came into Washington County for the purpose of sinking a well, causing something of a minor rush for Utah oil land. The mining of hydrocarbons, particularly Gilsonite, also increased after statehood. Asphaltum, bituminous sand, and other products of the hydrocarbon mines useful for road construction became more and more economic.[24]

Depression of 1907-8. The most severe event in Utah mining during these years was the financial panic of 1907. Many mines were so hurt by the depressed prices of silver, copper, lead, and zinc that they closed down or stayed open only a portion of the time. Silver alone dropped from 66.3¢ per ounce to 53.2¢ per ounce, and the total production of silver mines in 1908 was only 50 percent of what it had been just the year before. Coal and hydrocarbons were also produced in much smaller quantities, with most of these mines staying open an average of four days a week.[25] Fortunately, the depression was of brief duration, and, despite the severity of its effect upon the mines, production was again increasing at a normal rate within two years.

Manufacturing

Utah was not as advanced in manufacturing as was the nation

during the 1896-1910 period. Much of the manufacturing which did take place was of a relatively low order; that is, most of the profitable industries were based upon agricultural products or the mines. The manufacturing picture for 1890, 1899, and 1909 is given in table 1.7. Three industries—the smelting and refining of copper, the smelting and refining of lead, and the manufacture of beet sugar—predominate, but the data could not be shown separately without disclosing individual operations. We do know that lead smelting and refining added $1.73 million to the value of manufactures in 1910 and employed 1,546 wage earners. Fourth in importance were cars and general shop construction and repairs by railroad companies.

While Utah was not a manufacturing state, it did possess more factories in a greater variety than most of the mountain states. In several fields Utah easily held its own. In addition to the great smelters, of which mention has already been made because of their close connection with mining, important factories were established to refine salt and sugar, to make candy and can fruit, and to manufacture cloth and clothing.

Salt. The largest salt enterprise in Utah, the Inland Crystal Salt Company, was originally promoted in the 1880s by James Jack, treasurer of the LDS Church, possibly on behalf of the Church. The enterprise was sold to a Midwest syndicate in 1891, but controlling interest was later reacquired by the

TABLE 1.7
Manufactures in Utah: 1890, 1899, 1909

	1890	1899	1909
Number of establishments	531	575	749
Number of wage earners	4,349	5,413	11,785
Total wages	$2,191,265	$2,762,522	$8,399,634
Value added by manufacturing	$4,659,017	$6,541,398	$20,723,616

SOURCE: *Measures of Economic Changes in Utah,* pp. 80-88.

Church in 1897. The local capital in this enterprise amounted to some $60,000.[26] This enterprise produced some twenty thousand tons of evaporated solar salt in its plant on the shores of Great Salt Lake in 1900. Three smaller salt companies also had plants in the general area.

Sugar. Utah's first sugar plant was built at Lehi in 1891 by the Utah Sugar Company. By the late 1890s the company was operating in the black, employing more than one hundred hands to process thirty-six thousand tons of beets per season and creating additional income for six hundred farmers. In 1902 the founders sold a controlling interest to Henry O. Havemeyer, president of the monopolistic American Sugar Refining Company. The purpose of this sale was to acquire capital for expansion. Within a year the company doubled the capacity of the Lehi plant and erected a million-dollar factory at Garland in 1903. A rash of companies—partly through Church capital, partly through Havemeyer's capital, and partly through local capital—erected plants at Ogden, Logan, and Lewiston, Utah, and at Idaho Falls, Sugar City, Blackfoot, and Nampa, Idaho. Additional auxiliary plants to slice the beets before sending pulp and juice to the "mother" plant at Lehi were constructed in Provo, Springville, and Spanish Fork. Much of the sugar was exported. Under the leadership of Joseph F. Smith, David Eccles, and John C. Cutler, most of these plants were united in 1907 under the Utah-Idaho Sugar Company, a $13-million combination.[27]

Candy. A natural outgrowth of the sugar industry was the manufacture of candy, in which Utah developed a specialty early in the century. A related factor may have been the relatively small consumption of intoxicants. The J. G. McDonald Company was one of those which began to flourish during this period. It is also of significance that the brewery industry of Salt Lake Valley showed the promise which later was made manifest.

Canning. Although canning began relatively late in Utah because of the rural orientation of its people, the business expanded rapidly after its beginning in the late 1880s and 1890s. The first two canneries, established at Woods Cross and Ogden, began production around 1890. By 1910 the industry had grown to include fifty factories, producing about 750,000 cases of canned fruits and vegetables each year.[28] The manufacture of butter and cheese also became important during this period. This development was related, of course, to the growth of the dairy industry.

Textiles and clothing. Several woolen and cotton mills had been constructed by the pioneers in the 1860s and 1870s in various parts of the state, but none of these attained particular significance except the Provo Woolen Mills, the first large manufacturing establishment in Utah. This enterprise had a hard time during the depression of the 1890s but was back on its feet by the turn of the century, employing two hundred hands and producing an output varying between $250,000 and $300,000 a year. The election of its guiding light, Reed Smoot, to the United States Senate in 1904, its distance from consuming centers, and its obsolescent machinery caused the company to cease operations in 1904, and it remained idle until its purchase by the Knight Investment Company in 1910.

The most important clothing enterprise of the period had been initiated by Zion's Cooperative Mercantile Institution (ZCMI) in 1878. This factory turned out overalls, jumpers, lined coats and vests, overshirts, undershirts, and men's drawers. At the turn of the century, some 750,000 yards of denim and other material were being used in the production of an output valued at more than $100,000 per year.[29]

One interesting attempt was made in Utah during this period to encourage the manufacture of silk. A Utah Silk Commission was organized to lecture to interested persons on the care and feeding of silkworms and the best methods of winding and packing the silk. The added incentive of a bounty paid to persons producing a given amount of silk engendered considerable enthusiasm. In 1904 some 8,656 pounds were produced in the leading silk counties of Washington, Kane, and Box Elder. The silk industry did not seem to grow, despite some encouraging signs, and eventually it was abandoned as a state-supported industry.

Public Utilities

In 1893 a group of young Utahns, primarily Ogdenites, organized the Pioneer Electric Power Company to build a dam across Ogden River, ten miles east of the city in Ogden Canyon. The purposes of the dam were to create a huge reservoir of water for power, culinary, and irrigation purposes and to provide power for the city of Ogden, for the use of electric railways in Ogden and Salt Lake City, and for factories of every description in northern Utah. It was expected that up to twenty thousand acres of arid land in the northwestern part of Weber Valley could be irrigated with the surplus water stored in the eastern end of Ogden Canyon. This land was thought to be peculiarly adapted to the culture of sugar beets, and the company expected to establish a factory near Ogden to transform the beets into sugar. The depression of the 1890s prevented the immediate consummation of this project, but Joseph Banigan, a rubber manufacturer in Providence, Rhode Island, agreed to invest $1.5 million in the project, and a new company, The Pioneer Electric Power Company, was organized early in 1896. Several hundred men were employed, a long canal was dug from the dam site to west Ogden, and the dam was completed in 1898. A power plant with a capacity of ten thousand horsepower was completed in 1897. The construction, whose story cannot be detailed here, was a major engineering achievement and was directed by Charles K. Bannister. The construction of the electric line to Salt Lake City was unprecedented in American engineering. Designed to work at fifteen thousand volts, this was the first long-distance transmission from a man-made dam especially constructed to generate electricity.

When its facilities were completed in 1897, the company merged with the Salt Lake and Ogden Gas and Electric Light Company, the Citizens' Electric Light Company, and the Big Cottonwood Power Company—all of which had been providing gas and electrical service in Salt Lake City—to form the Union Light & Power Company. This company was capitalized at $4.5 million, with the controlling interest in the hands of the LDS Church. Union Light & Power was the most extensive and complete system for the distribution of electrical energy and power over a wide area in the United States. It embraced the Salt Lake and Weber valleys and owned two hundred miles of overhead line construction. The company was not a financial success, however, and in 1899 was reorganized with a scaled-down bonded indebtedness, and a new company was created called the Utah Light and Power Company. Caught up in the tide of McKinley prosperity, the Utah Light and Power Company was increasingly profitable. The company later added additional properties and in 1904 formed the Utah Light and Railway Company. This gave it a working monopoly on all street railways in Salt Lake City and Ogden and all electrical generating facilities in Weber, Davis, and Salt Lake counties. With a capitalization of $10 million, it was the largest corporation formed in Utah until the incorporation of the Utah-Idaho Sugar Company. In 1906 the controlling interest was sold to Edward H. Harriman, principal owner of the Union Pacific Railroad. The company eventually became a part of the Utah Power and Light Company.[30]

Railroads

As a railroad center between California and the East, Utah enjoyed a good deal of railroad expansion and activity. Although the railroad threw teamsters out of work and caused occasional failures in small industry, it gave impetus to commercial farming and mining and reduced the cost of machinery and other manufactured goods.

During the 1880s and 1890s, the Union Pacific Railroad had a virtual monopoly on railway transportation, and many felt that the company "took advantage of its monopolistic position to impose highly discriminatory freight rates on many commodities. . . . "[31] Although a few independent lines were in operation to and from the larger mines, these were also dependent on U.P. for transportation out of the state. The monopoly of Union Pacific finally brought about such resentment that determined attempts were made to break it by building competing lines. The most determined of these efforts was made by

Senator William A. Clark of Montana, who organized the Salt Lake, San Pedro, and Los Angeles Railroad in 1900. This company began to acquire a right-of-way for a road from Salt Lake to Los Angeles and furnished a definite challenge to the new road being built by Union Pacific (as part of the Oregon Short Line system) which would follow the same route. The Utah and Pacific, as the U.P. road was called, was already under construction when the Salt Lake line was begun.

Both roads began construction east of the Nevada line, building parallel on the same disputed grade. Fighting broke out at construction sites among workers for both lines, and the matter finally reached the courts of Nevada. After a great deal of litigation, a compromise was made, and the two lines were built running parallel down the Meadow Valley wash. The denouement came when Senator Clark triumphantly announced that the Salt Lake line had completed negotiations for the transfer of Short Line property to his railroad, and connections were being completed to Los Angeles. Through trains began running on the Salt Lake, San Pedro, and Los Angeles line in 1903. The line was later incorporated into the Union Pacific System.

The Oregon Short Line, one of the biggest and most active railroads during this period, had an interesting history. The road was originally in competition with Union Pacific, with 1,421 miles of track in Utah, Idaho, Montana, Wyoming, and Oregon and with head offices in Salt Lake City.[32] In 1897 the Short Line allowed the Rio Grande Western and other lines to invade Union Pacific territory on an equal footing with U.P., which connected with the Short Line at Granger. Union Pacific retaliated by canceling tariff and car service to the Oregon Short Line. Peace was restored in 1899, and the next year the OSL became virtually a part of the Union Pacific complex.

One of the most interesting improvements made on the Oregon Short Line was a line which became known as the Lucin Cutoff. Commenced in 1899 and completed in 1900, the cutoff ran from Ogden west over level country for fifteen miles to the Great Salt Lake, where the line ran on trestles across the lake. This cutoff saved a great deal of time for the railroad on that run and was regarded as a great feat of engineering.

At the end of the first decade of the twentieth century, Salt Lake City was a great railroad center. With the Southern Pacific line to San Francisco, the Short Line to Portland, the Salt Lake route to Los Angeles, a Western Pacific route to San Francisco, and the transcontinental routes to Chicago, Minneapolis, and St. Paul, Salt Lake was well on its way to becoming a leading center of trade and transportation in the West.

Banking

The growing financial importance of Utah, its increasing importance in business, and its growing "commerciality" are all reflected in the growth of banking. In 1896 Utah had twelve national banks and thirty-four private and state banks, most of which had been organized in the 1880s. By this time, banks were located not only in Salt Lake City and Ogden, but also in many cities throughout the state. Because of the depression of the 1890s, there was little financial activity in the state until after the turn of the century. Several banks were organized during the first decade of the twentieth century, particularly after 1905. In that year, ten state banks, one private bank, and two national banks were added to those already in existence. This continued at a similar rate in 1906, 1908 (1907 was a crisis year), 1909, and 1910. By the end of 1910 there were seventy-eight state and private banks in Utah and twenty-four national banks. This was more than double the number of banks in 1896.[33]

Further evidence of the commercialization of the economy—the adaptation of the state to the monetary economy— by 1910 was that in 1908 the LDS Church abandoned its traditional policy of requiring that tithing be paid in kind and, instead, placed tithing on a cash basis. Moreover, by this time the stores and factories, which had been accustomed to paying their help partly in cash and partly in "store goods" or "factory goods," had given up the scrip system and gone entirely over to cash.

Summary

To summarize, the principal economic events in Utah during the period 1896 to 1910 were these:

1. The initiation of the Pioneer Electric Power project in Ogden Canyon in 1896, which precipitated Utah's important hydroelectric power industry.

2. Sale of Utah Sugar Company to Henry Havemeyer and the American Sugar Refining Company in 1902, thus bringing to Utah the capital with which to expand the Lehi plant and to build other plants, rendering permanent the important beet sugar industry.

3. The approval for the Strawberry Valley Project in 1903, thus originating the first, and one of the largest, reclamation projects in Utah's history.

4. The formation of the Utah Copper Company in 1903, thus launching an enterprise that was to develop the low-grade porphyry ores of "the richest hole on earth," from which $7 billion in ores have since been removed.

5. Completion of the Salt Lake, San Pedro, and Los Angeles Railroad in 1906, thus giving rise to the important trade with California which has been a basic feature of Utah's economy ever since.

2. The Burgeoning of Utah's Economy: 1910–18

Thomas G. Alexander

The nineteenth-century mining industry produced income figures giving the Mountain West the appearance, at least, of unusual abundance. Although significantly below the national average in urban-industrial growth, the region exceeded the national level in per capita income. Utah, however, did not follow the regional trend because of heavy reliance on agriculture and marginal manufacturing and because of poor access to market . During the first decades of the twentieth century the remainder of the Mountain West became more like Utah as agriculture surpassed mining in the various local economies. At the same time, the Pacific Coast states, which had been economically much like the Mountain West in the nineteenth century, passed the threshold of urban-industrial development.[1]

Agricultural Expansion

In the decade from 1910 to 1920, agriculture was the mainstay of Utah's economy. Although total rural population continued to decline relative to urban population, it enjoyed an absolute increase of 16.7 percent, from about 200,000 to almost 234,000 persons, while the rate of urban growth actually slowed below that of the previous decade. During the decade the total number of farms increased from 21,700 to 25,700, and total agricultural acreage increased from 3.4 million to 5.0 million. In 1920, 9.6 percent of the total area of Utah was taken for farming.[2]

Almost all areas of the agricultural economy benefited from the good times. Under the stimulus of high prices and reduced freight rates, fruit crop acreage increased until in 1912 Utah farmers owned more than forty-three thousand acres. Markets became glutted by 1915, however, and farmers began to pull up large numbers of trees.[3] Field-, truck-, and grain-crop acreage—unlike horticulture—continued to increase during the decade. Although superior varieties of seeds were not introduced into Utah before 1900 and in some areas not until 1915, the development of better grades of wheat, especially strains such as Turkey Red, made the Utah product more easily marketable.[4]

Although the area of most intense farming remained along the Wasatch Front during the decade between 1910 and 1920, farmers pushed into hitherto sparsely cultivated regions. An increase in the number of farms took place in each county except Grand, Juab, Morgan, and Wasatch. The largest percentage growth came in Iron and San Juan counties.[5] Population growth, caused presumably by people taking up land on the recently opened Uintah and Ouray Indian reservation lands, necessitated the organization of Duchesne County in 1915 and Daggett County in 1918.[6]

By amendments to the Homestead Act, the federal government also promoted land acquisition. Changes in the law in 1909 and 1912 allowed farmers to take 320 acres of land for dry farming after a three-year residence, and the 1916 Stockraising Homestead Act granted full sections for homesteads.[7]

With the increased interest in land acquisition, new real estate companies sprang into existence. Of five real estate corporations listed in Hogle's handbook in 1917, the four for which dates of incorporation are given were founded after 1910. In the nine years between 1909 and 1918, settlers entered an average of 575,000 new acres each year.[8]

Between 1914 and 1916 Edgar B. Brossard of the Utah State Agricultural Experiment Station made an extensive study of farming conditions at various irrigated farms throughout Utah.[9] The farms in Hyde Park, although somewhat smaller than the state average, were typical. Farmers planted slightly more winter wheat in 1916 than in 1914 because the price increased more than it did for other crops, and dry farming was extended to lands formerly used for grazing. Farmers usually grew sugar beets on about ten acres of their best land. Although potatoes were easier to grow, the sugar beets produced a higher cash return, they did not have to compete on distant markets, and contracts with sugar companies insured a steady income. A few of the farmers ran cattle on the Cache National Forest, but grazing permits were difficult to obtain, and livestock raising was not sufficiently profitable to give up field crops. On the average farm, sugar beets were the main source of income, milk and dairy products stood second, and potatoes and garden crops placed third. Farmers had generally invested about $420 each in modern farm machinery as against the Utah average of $449 in 1914. Farm tenancy was great neither in Hyde Park nor in Utah as a whole.

One of the major problems of Utah farmers was the relative isolation of the state and the consequent high cost of shipping long distances to major markets. This produced a condition in which the prices of exported crops such as hay, wheat, barley, sugar beets, and potatoes were lower in Utah than the national average; and the prices of corn, oats, and rye were higher. Most fruit crops had to be consumed near home because such Utah fruits as peaches, having to compete with products of areas such as southern Michigan, remained at a disadvantage owing to long transportation distances. During the period before the United States' entry into World War I, however, the development of canneries and creameries widened the market for many crops and products.[10]

The life of the farmer was comparatively pleasant during the decade. From 1909 to 1918 monthly pay for farmhands without board increased 50 percent, from about fifty-six dollars to eighty-four dollars. The income of the farm family in the late teens ranged from $2,200 to $2,300 per year. Most farm homes within fifty miles of the railroad had electric lighting and other conveniences, but those beyond were without indoor plumbing or electric lights and were not far removed from pioneer conditions. In Utah, where the majority of farm families lived in the Wasatch Front counties, most lived fairly well.[11]

Part of the prosperity of southern Utah Valley came from the Strawberry Valley reclamation project, which the government authorized in December 1905.[12] By November 1912 crews working on the Strawberry tunnel had drilled through, and they completed cement work in 1913. Workmen finished the Highline canal, which reached from the Spanish Fork River to Payson, in 1916 and began work on the canal to Mapleton and Springville in 1918. Work on the dam started in 1911 and was fully completed in 1917. The first project water was delivered in June 1915.

The supply of water and power to southern Utah County helped promote the economic development of the area. Beet sugar companies built plants, and businessmen erected alfalfa mills and vining stations. Until 1910 Juab and Sanpete counties had grown at about the same rate as the project area. In 1915 population spurted forward, and southern Utah County began to flourish and develop. The growth of adjoining counties, however, was limited by lack of water. In 1915 the assessed valuation of property in the project area was $7.5 million; by 1920 it had grown to $26.9 million.

Sugar beets. Possibly the securest portion of the agricultural picture was the beet sugar industry. The price of sugar was fairly stable until the beginning of World War I, when it began to rise. It climbed to seven dollars per ton in 1917 and twelve dollars by 1920. Although the crop required intensive farming, it provided summer work for children and meant that the farmer did not need as much land to produce a good living. In 1917 more than nine thousand farmers engaged in sugar beet raising, and factories turned out $11.1 million worth of sugar products. In 1920 the sugar produced was worth $28 million.[13]

It is difficult to separate the agricultural phase of the sugar beet industry from its manufacturing sector. Owing to a favorable combination of soil, available water, and climate, Utah farmers became successful beet cultivators.[14] The processing of the beet in Utah came about because of the great loss in processed weight, which made it cheaper to ship the finished product than the raw material. Close cooperation between the company and the farmer developed, and production fitted in well with the farmer's other activities because weeding and thinning were completed before haying was underway. The harvest came later in the fall when other crops were already in. During the late fall and winter many farmers became industrial workers in local sugar factories.[15]

The period after 1910 was one of expansion for the manufacturing end of the industry as well as for beet farming. Between 1910 and 1919 a number of new plants opened in various towns of central and northern Utah. By 1915 the industry was second in the manufacturing field only to metal processing. In 1916 Utah moved into third place in sugar production in the United States.[16] The prosperity of the companies reflected this development. In April 1914 the stock of the Utah-Idaho Sugar Company sold at seven dollars per share, or three dollars below par value. Within thirty months, the value had increased more than 400 percent, and in November 1916 it was being traded at twenty-nine dollars per share.[17]

During this period of expansion, beet sugar companies bore the brunt of considerable adverse comment. Critics pointed out in 1913, for instance, that Utah sugar sold in Texas for $4.15 per one hundred pounds while Utah citizens had to pay $5.25. During the First World War, a growers' organization charged that the United States Food Administration, in collusion with the state administrator and the companies, had set the price of beets at such a low level that the farmers were losing profits to the company. They pointed out that payments to growers in European countries averaged several dollars per ton more than in the United States.[18]

Meat packing. In addition to the sugar industry, a number of other industries, such as meat packing, were based on the primary processing of Utah and intermountain state agricultural products. Until well after 1900 Denver was the westernmost livestock market between the midwestern and the Pacific Coast states. In 1906 the Ogden Packing and Provision Company built a small plant, and by 1914 two packing houses were in operation there. They furnished employment to 130 people and produced $1.9 million worth of dressed animals.[19]

After the outbreak of the war, Utah's meat packing industry

began to expand more rapidly. The Ogden Packing and Provision Company grew until in 1916 it alone employed 240 people and sold $3 million in products. In 1917, with money invested by Utah and Idaho capitalists, including Fred J. Kiesel, James Pingree, Adam Patterson, Lars Hansen, and Charles and Simon S. Jensen, it expanded until it had the largest packing plant west of Omaha. In 1916 the Cudahy Packing Company purchased the Inter-Mountain Packing Company plant in North Salt Lake and remodeled it to an increased capacity. The estimated product value of the industry in 1918 was $8.3 million.[20]

Still, by 1918 representatives of the industry were not satisfied with the progress of their business. Utah was far below its potential in cattle raising. It was nearly the lowest in the mountain states in livestock per square mile—7.6 compared with Wyoming's 13.2 and Idaho's 34.8. Simon S. Jensen of the Ogden Packing and Provision Company pointed out that it was not unusual to see a trainload of cattle, followed by a trainload of grain, followed by a trainload of hay—all going to the same place. He said that bankers were not generally inclined to lend money to livestock growers even though farmers needed credit in the winter so they would not have to sell their partly matured cattle. Another difficulty was that freight rates favored live animals over dressed meats. Representatives of the industry petitioned the Federal Trade Commission to force the railroads to change the rates, but by late 1918 they had achieved no success.[21]

To serve these newly developed packing facilities, other services were provided. The Associated Press began quoting livestock prices on the Salt Lake City and Ogden markets in 1916. In the same year the Salt Lake Union Stock Yards Company took over and expanded the former Inter-Mountain Packing Company yards, and the Ogden Union Stock Yards Company completed new lots at Ogden. As the war continued, Ogden became an important center for shipping, feeding, and marketing of livestock. During the year 1919 the Ogden Union Stockyards handled shipments of three thousand to seven thousand animals per day.[22]

Milling. The war also served to stimulate the milling industry, which by the time of the United States' entry into the war supplied Utah's mining regions and the urban centers of the intermountain states as well as part of the Los Angeles market. In addition, the United States Food Administration opened a channel leading to Galveston and New Orleans. The increased emphasis on better strains of wheat and low costs owing to the use of hydroelectric power helped considerably in the industry's growth. Utah's milling industry, centered in Ogden, had by December 1919 become one of the ten leading milling centers of the United States. Utah became a net exporter of flour, but it was an importer of cereals in the form of breakfast food and other commodities. There was, however, some expansion of cereal plants and bakeries in Utah during the decade.[23]

Canning. Ogden also became Utah's important canning center. Fully half of the thirty-two canneries located in the state in 1914 were found in the Junction City. In 1914 Utah's canning factories produced a total of 1.3 million cases of fruits and vegetables, and Utah ranked fifth among the states in canning. Although the outbreak of the European war slowed development momentarily, the industry soon expanded, and in 1917 twenty-two Ogden canning factories secured government contracts. One of them, the Everfresh Food Company, had such a great need for canning produce that it made a standing offer to take all garden truck in lots of ten pounds or more. The mining camps and stock ranges of the West, under the stimulation of wartime conditions, were also heavy purchasers. In 1918 the value of Utah's product was $3.4 million, of which 64 percent was sold outside the state.[24]

Textiles. Another industry based upon the products of Utah, although in a roundabout way, was the woolen and textile industry. Most of the woolen mills were interested in supplying miners and workmen with products of utility rather than making products of beauty. The market was especially good in the mining camps of New Mexico and Arizona and in the lumber camps of the Pacific Coast, where route salesmen employed by each factory sold "black Mormon underwear." Partly because of unfavorable freight rates, Utah had no scouring plants.

Wools sheared in Utah were shipped to the East, scoured, dyed black, then shipped back again. Two large concerns, John Scowcroft and Sons of Ogden and ZCMI of Salt Lake City, produced overalls for miners and construction workers, although most cotton products were made on a special-order basis.[25]

Other consumption goods. Another industry of importance which involved the secondary manufacture of a Utah product was candy making. In 1915, $2.4 million worth of candy made in Utah was sold in the West and throughout the world. Regular shipments went to Australia, Japan, and Alaska. The largest plants were the J. G. McDonald Chocolate Company and the Sweet Candy Company of Salt Lake City, the Shupe-Williams Candy Company of Ogden, and the Startup Candy Company of Provo. By 1920 sales ran to $5 million per year.[26]

Prohibition, which Utah instituted in August 1917, had different effects on various industries. Soda water bottlers noted an increase in sales as local firms which had formerly produced malt beverages turned to soft drinks. Conversely, the liquor distillers and the cigar makers suffered. Saloons, which had handled the cigars until Prohibition, went out of business, and chain stores coming into the state at the time pushed eastern goods in Ogden and Salt Lake City, where the major cigar market had been. The major protection for the Utah industry, which was based partly on Utah-grown tobacco, was the high shipping cost.[27]

Industrial Growth

Manufacturing. In addition to the expansion of the agricultural processing industries, the First World War was undoubtedly responsible for most of the growth in heavy manufacturing in Utah. If Ogden was the state's food processing center, Salt Lake City, with fully one-half of Utah's manufacturing establishments in 1911, served as the focus of industry. As a result of wartime production needs, the first attempt at the fabrication of iron and steel since 1883 occurred in 1915 just south of Salt Lake City at the plant of the Utah Iron and Steel Company in Midvale. Scrap was the principal source of metal, and fuel for its

150-ton open-hearth furnace came from gas made from Sunnyside coal. Although the plant was basically a war industry, it manufactured rails, which it sold principally in western mining districts. An electric furnace was installed for the refining of a superior grade of steel. By the end of 1916 one hundred men worked at the plant, and plans were being laid to increase the capacity of the furnaces to produce three thousand tons of steel daily. During 1918 Utah produced propellers for ships on a government contract, and plans were laid for reopening the iron deposits of Iron County.[28]

Prosperity in the mining industry gave rise to the plant which the Hercules Powder Company completed at Bacchus, about fifteen miles west of Salt Lake City, in 1915. The company constructed a village of thirty dwellings, a hotel, clubhouse, library, dance hall, general store, and schoolhouse. The plant employed 115 men by 1916; they turned out 800,000 pounds of high explosives per year.[29]

The most important manufacturing adjunct of the mining industry was smelting and refining. By 1910 the industry had developed to a respectable size, with six great smelters representing an investment of more than $20 million. Indicative of the economy involved in the large-scale operation of the Utah Copper Company is the fact that, whereas in 1872 the cost for mining and smelting high-grade ores was $89 per ton, by 1913 the cost of handling low-grade porphyry ores was $1.25 per ton. As the price of metals rose, even before the war, it became profitable to smelt old slag and tailings at the mines.[30]

Smelting during most of the decade was a highly profitable business, inducing the International Smelting and Refining Company to break ground for a lead smelter at Tooele in 1911. Plants in Utah refined ores of all types from local mines in the Coeur d' Alene district of Idaho and in Nevada, Montana, and Arizona. Although there was a slump from 1912 to 1915, the war stimulated the smelting industry to such an extent that by 1919 Utah had the greatest smelting district in North America. In 1919 Salt Lake Valley smelters treated 4.43 million tons of metal. Anaconda, Montana, and Douglas, Arizona, each processed more copper, but the Salt Lake area plants treated more combined metal.[31]

A start was made toward a chemical industry in Utah in 1912. In that year sulfuric acid was recovered from copper smelting. In 1916 the Utah Copper Company, in conjunction with the Garfield Smelting Company, organized the Garfield Chemical and Manufacturing Corporation to construct and operate an acid plant near the Garfield smelter. The original capacity was seventy-five tons per day, but this was increased to 150 tons.[32]

If manufacturing did not become as important in Utah as in the nation as a whole, it did nevertheless grow more rapidly in Utah during the decade from 1910 to 1920 than in the rest of the country. It also grew more rapidly than did agriculture. In 1910 approximately 28.3 percent of Utah's labor force was engaged in agriculture, as against 11.9 percent in manufacturing. In 1920, 28.9 percent was engaged in agriculture and 14.5 percent in manufacturing. The greatest percentage increases came in employment in the processing of food products and in the manufacture of iron and steel and machinery products. This increase made the iron and steel products sector almost as large an employer as mining by 1920.[33]

Minerals. Mining, paced by copper, was extremely important to the economy. Production of copper increased from 109 million pounds in 1909 to 246 million in 1917. The industry seems to have received its major shot in the arm from the merger of the Utah Copper Corporation and the Boston Consolidated Copper Company in 1910; this merger combined the leadership of Daniel C. Jackling and the financial acumen of the Guggenheims. From about 1907 to 1909 the mineral industry suffered a slight setback because of the commercial depression; beginning in 1910 the rise continued with only slight pauses until the end of World War I. At the outbreak of the war in August 1914 a decline in the copper industry forced a 50 percent curtailment in operations. In spite of the cutback, however, dividends in 1914 were still higher at $7.4 million than the $5.7 million paid in 1913. Conditions began to improve in March 1915, and the industry moved to a new record for that year. In 1916 profits for the company rose to $33.7 million. Utah copper noted some difficulties after the United States' entry into the war which it had not experienced before. As a result of the draft, a serious shortage of competent labor developed, and therefore labor costs rose. The company, nevertheless, remained in excellent condition until the end of the war.[34]

In addition to copper, lead—with a 123-million-pound production in 1910—was an important mineral industry. The major producer of lead, accounting for almost one-third of the annual output, was the Park City district. Bingham and Tintic stood second and third. Lead mining was closely allied with the extraction of silver and zinc. Actually, the only way producers could profit from processing lead was through the simultaneous recovery of silver. As a result, lead producers were very much afraid of the lower duties imposed by the Underwood-Simmons Tariff of 1913, but the war stimulated the market for most base metals to new records. In 1916 Utah stood second in the United States in silver production, third in lead, and fourth in copper.[35]

The war affected the gold market much less than it did that of other metals. Before the war, the largest producers of gold were Bingham, Tintic, and Mercur. Until Bingham forged ahead in gold production as a by-product of its copper recovery, the Tintic district had led the state in production. The state's gold production dropped somewhat during the decade, owing partly to the closing of the mines at Mercur. By 1912 gold extraction at Mercur averaged only one-eighth of an ounce of gold per ton of ore, and the mines had to cease operations in the next year.[36]

A number of nonmetallic mineral industries were also active during the period. Two companies engaged in the production of salt on Great Salt Lake. The Salduro salt deposits near the Western Pacific Railroad line close to the Nevada border were opened. Other nonmetallic minerals mined during the period included native bitumens, gypsum, dolomite, potash, and limestone, which was used in sugar refining. With the exception of Gilsonite, salt, and potash, the commercial development of the nonmetallics depended upon markets within the state. Except insofar as these local markets were stimulated, production was largely unaffected by the war.[37]

As a result of the closing of shipping lanes from Germany, the potash industry developed extensively during the war. The price of potash rose from thirty-five dollars per ton to five hundred dollars per ton after the blockade of Germany began in 1914, and development was initiated at almost every potash deposit in the United States. Deposits of alunite were opened about seven miles southwest of Marysvale; the Solvay Process Company built a plant at Salduro, Utah, about twenty miles east of Wendover, to extract the mineral from Great Salt Lake; and the Salt Lake Chemical Company, a subsidiary of the Diamond Match Company, began operations near Grantsville. After the end of the war, production began to decline under German competition and was terminated by 1921.[38]

Another mineral industry which the war promoted was coal mining. A group of independent companies fought hard with the dominant Utah Fuel Company and succeeded in cutting it to about 40 percent of the market by 1916. Although automatic machinery was introduced, employment increased steadily through the early twenties. Under the stimulus of advancing wartime conditions, the volume of coal mined increased until in 1920 six million tons were produced.[39]

Banking. The development of commerce, industry, mining, and agriculture which took place during the period also promoted the growth of banking. In 1910 there were 102 banks in Utah. By 1919 this number had grown to 123, but more impressive still, total assets grew from $44.2 million in 1910 to $102.6 million in December 1919. Also, through the efforts of Utah and southern Idaho bankers, led by the Salt Lake Clearing House Association, the Federal Reserve Bank of San Francisco located a branch in Salt Lake City.[40]

Transportation, communication, and utilities. As agriculture, mining, and manufacturing pushed to new heights, transportation, communication, and utilities underwent a relatively steady growth. The bulk of those employed in transportation worked Utah's railroad industry. The Southern Pacific was the leading employer in Ogden, with an annual payroll in 1918 of more than $1 million and an employment of about one thousand. In August 1910, the steam railroad network was essentially completed by the construction of the Western Pacific to San Francisco. The Bamberger railroad was electrified in 1910, and electric interurban lines were built south of Salt Lake City to Payson between 1914 and 1916 and north from Ogden to Logan and on to Preston, Idaho, from 1914 to 1918. A number of narrow-gauge lines were completed to serve mines at Ophir, Alta, and Bingham, and by 1918 the value of Utah's 3,255 miles of steam and electric railroads totaled $92 million.[41]

Although the railroads were important to Utah's economy, their policies may have actually inhibited the development of other industries. Shipping rates, for instance, favored live animals and raw materials going east; that policy surely retarded the development of sounder industries in many fields. On the other hand, the pricing policies of the railroad helped the beet sugar industry compete in other areas, although they also caused Utahns to pay higher prices for their sugar than they normally would have and perhaps retarded secondary use of sugar in the processing of fruits and in the manufacturing of candy and confectionery.[42]

Another phase of communication which received a boost during the decade was the telephone industry. The Rocky Mountain Bell Telephone Company—which had rights to serve Idaho, Montana, Utah, and Wyoming—became part of the Mountain States Telephone and Telegraph Company in July 1911. A new era in communications opened on July 28, 1914, when crews set the last pole and spliced wires at Wendover, Utah, to connect the first transcontinental telephone line.[43]

Also indicative of the progress of the utilities during the period is the development of the Utah Power and Light Company. Incorporated in 1912 from a number of smaller utilities, the company supplied service by 1922 to 205 communities in an area bounded by Ashton, Idaho, on the north and Huntington, Utah, 370 miles to the south. The utility operated forty generating stations with a total capacity of 224,000 horsepower, of which 200,000 was hydroelectric, mostly derived from the Bear River. The corporation employed three thousand people with an annual payroll of $3 million. Demand for power increased and changed during the period. Formerly electricity was used mainly for lighting, but industry came to use more power in processing goods. The number of customers of Utah Power and Light grew from 39,700 in 1912 to more than 83,000 in 1922.[44]

Urbanization

The development of manufacturing, transportation, and communication helped promote the growth of Utah's urban centers (see table 2.1). Between 1900 and 1910 urban areas increased by 64 percent to 172,934 people, or 46 percent of the population. Urban expansion slowed somewhat during the following decade to 24.7 percent; but in 1920, 215,584 people, or 48 percent of the population, lived in cities. This slower development was probably a function of both the low base in 1900 and the number of people who remained in agriculture or moved to farms during the prosperous wartime period. In spite of the slow urban growth, the population of Utah's cities increased greatly (see table 2.2). Salt Lake City, with a population of 92,777 in 1910, increased to 118,110 in 1920. Ogden grew from 25,580 to 32,804 people, and Provo and Logan showed increases of a similar degree.[45]

With this growth came a considerable change to the cities. The face of Salt Lake City, especially, underwent a tremendous transformation. Beginning in 1909, the mining magnate Samuel Newhouse constructed the twin Newhouse and Boston buildings on the east side of Main Street between Third and Fourth South. In 1911 the Hotel Utah was built, the Walker Bank Building was constructed in 1912, and the Hotel Newhouse was built in 1915. The federal building, originally constructed in 1905, was extended in 1911, and in 1917 The Church of Jesus Christ of Latter-day Saints completed its office building.[46]

Largely owing to the million-dollar inheritance tax paid by the heirs of E. H. Harriman and David Eccles and a million-dollar bond issue, the state constructed its capitol building between 1912 and 1915. Richard K. A. Kletting of Salt Lake City secured the contract as architect in March 1912, and ground-breaking ceremonies took place on December 16. James

TABLE 2.1
Changes in Urban and Rural Population in Utah, 1890-1930

	Urban Total	Percentage	Percentage of Increase	Rural Total	Percentage	Percentage of Increase
1890	75,155	35.7	123.2	135,624	64.3	23.0
1900	105,427	38.1	40.3	171,322	61.9	26.3
1910	172,934	46.3	64.0	200,417	53.7	17.0
1920	215,584	48.0	24.7	233,812	52.0	16.7
1930	266,264	52.4	23.5	241,583	47.6	3.3

SOURCE: J. R. Mahoney, "Measure of Economic Changes in Utah, 1847-1947," *Utah Economic and Business Review* 7 (December 1947): 13.

Stewart and Company of New York and Salt Lake City were awarded the initial contract for $1.1 million, but more than $2.7 million was actually spent on the structure and its decorations. The Consolidated Stone Company's quarry in Little Cottonwood Canyon, east of Salt Lake City, furnished stone for the edifice.[47]

Reform legislation. As a response to industrial and urban growth, the period after 1900 on both the national and state levels was one of economic reform. The Wilson administration, which began in 1913, culminated the development in the nation, and the decade from 1910 to 1920 witnessed a great deal of economic reform in Utah. Utah put into effect a nine-hour law for women in 1911 and a minimum-wage law for the fair sex in 1913, both of which were enforced by the Bureau of Immigration, Labor, and Statistics, the forerunner of the Industrial Commission. Most employers supported this legislation, and by 1914, although some employees had lost their jobs because of the laws, they were generally accepted.[48]

Other industrial reform legislation included the Child Labor Act of 1911. This law provided that no boy or girl under fourteen could be employed in any establishment where poisonous or dangerous materials were used, and no boy under fourteen or girl under sixteen could be required to work more than fifty-four hours in any week. No girls or women were to be employed in any place where intoxicating liquor was sold, and no boy under twelve nor girl under sixteen, except under some conditions, was allowed to sell newspapers on the streets of cities of the first or second class.

There was considerable pressure to regulate public utilities, to enforce adherence to safety regulations in industry, to insure workmen against injuries caused by industrial accidents, and to allow employees the right to organize. Both governors William Spry, a Republican, and Simon Bamberger, a Democrat, called for various pieces of such legislation. In 1911 the state established a relief fund for firemen and in 1915 organized a commission to examine the need for a law affecting the liability of employers for accidents. A report was submitted to the state legislature on the basis of which the 1917 legislature created an

TABLE 2.2
Population of Major Cities in Utah, 1900-1920

1900			1910			1920		
City	Population	Percentage of Increase	City	Population	Percentage of Increase	City	Population	Percentage of Increase
Salt Lake City	53,531	19.4	Salt Lake City	92,777	73.3	Salt Lake City	118,110	27.3
Ogden	16,313	9.6	Ogden	25,580	56.8	Ogden	32,804	28.2
Provo	6,185	19.9	Provo	8,925	44.3	Provo	10,303	15.4
Logan	5,451	19.4	Logan	7,522	38.0	Logan	9,439	25.5

SOURCE: Mahoney, p. 10.

industrial commission which took over the duties of the Commissioner of Immigration, Labor, and Statistics, the State Mine Inspectors, and the State Board of Conciliation and Arbitration. As part of the legislation, employers were required to insure their employees against accidents. In 1917 the state also established a commission to regulate public utilities, recognized unions as legal organizations, and limited the right of employers to secure injunctions in labor disputes. In 1911 and 1913 the state passed legislation regulating banks, and in 1919 the State Securities Commission was established.

The state of Utah also enacted some tax reform legislation during the decade. In 1911 the legislature provided for the appointment of a board of commissioners to review the system of taxation and revenue collection and to recommend changes in the law. Much property in the state was found to be inequitably assessed. Railroad holdings in Box Elder County, for instance, were assessed at $8.5 million; in Weber County, the major railroad center, assessors valued them at only $4.4 million; and in Salt Lake County, where facilities were inferior to those in Weber, they were estimated at $8.1 million. The legislatures did not act on the proposals in 1913 and 1915, apparently because of the lobbying efforts of individual and corporate interests. But in 1919 the state passed laws relating to taxation and the State Board of Equalization and changed the system of assessment of the property of industries. Metal mines were to be taxed on the basis of the value of their improvements plus three times their net proceeds. The assessed valuation of metal mines stood at $100 million, or about 15 percent of the total assessed valuation of the state in 1919, as against $46 million in 1918.[49]

The legislature also enacted some agrarian reform legislation. An act in 1913 created a State Board of Sheep Commissioners to try to control diseases and improve the quality of sheep. In 1919 the legislature authorized the State Board of Loan Commissioners to negotiate a loan for $1 million and to cooperate with the federal government in the reclamation of public lands for the settlement of ex-servicemen and other U.S. citizens.

The people of Utah also attempted to encourage the development of education in the state. In 1911 voters approved a constitutional amendment creating a high school fund, which by the school year 1915-16 amounted to $101,000. Before the creation of the fund, public high schools in Utah had been almost nonexistent. The 1915 legislature passed a law which made consolidation of county high schools mandatory. In 1913 the state established a School of Mines and five scholarships of $720 per year for graduates who showed aptitude for research at the University of Utah. The school considered a number of mining problems, including the development of low-grade ores.[50]

A Decade of Prosperity

With the new extensive economic development through the decade came also a period of "good times" for the people of Utah. Between 1900 and 1920 per capita income in Utah had increased from $183 to $556, which was a more rapid increase than that of the United States as a whole. However, Utahns ended the period more than one hundred dollars behind the national per capita income, whereas they had been only twenty dollars behind in 1900. In terms of 1964 dollars, Utahns earned $1,023 per capita in 1920. The per worker income in Utah was actually greater than the United States average, but larger families nullified part of the advantage.[51]

Working conditions during the decade from 1910 to 1920 were quite favorable. By 1916 violations of the minimum-wage and nine-hour laws for women were infrequent. Some industries which hired principally women were exemplary in the provision of excellent conditions for their workers. This was especially true of the J. G. McDonald Chocolate Company of Salt Lake City. This organization provided model dining and reading rooms, recreation facilities, an elegant roof garden, and a small zoo for the benefit of its employees.[52]

Perhaps because of the increase in wages over the period, the decade was notably free of strikes. In Salt Lake City and Ogden the skilled craftsmen as well as some common laborers were fairly well organized, but outside the cities labor was practically unorganized. The worst strike took place at Bingham in 1912, when the Western Federation of Miners tried to obtain recognition and higher wages. At the time of the strike the wage scale stood at $2.00 per day for surface workers, $2.50 for muckers, and $3.00 for miners. The union asked for fifty-cent-per-day increases, but the company offered only twenty-five-cent increases for muckers and miners. During the five-month strike, sheriff's deputies and immigrant strikebreakers were brought in.[53]

Wage scales as early as 1912 were generally above the nationwide average. In 1916 demand for workmen in the building trades was greater than the supply, and wages advanced an average of twenty-five cents to seventy-five cents per day. As the price of copper and other metals rose under wartime pressure, advances in wages resulted. In December 1916 employees at the Magna and Arthur plants of the Utah Copper Company received an increase in wages to about $3.25 per day, and miners received increases which brought their wages up to $4.50 per day. These increases were somewhat counterbalanced by inflation, but it seems apparent that workers fared better than they had before.[54]

The only major problem came in the metal industries in 1919, when the demand for metals began to decrease. Plants closed down or went on short hours. Wages were reduced an average of fifty to seventy-five cents per day in February. Although they returned to the former scale in July, it appears that many lost jobs or went on part-time status.[55]

The period from 1910 through 1918 was one of unprecedented prosperity for Utah. It is true that at the outbreak of the war in Europe the economy experienced a slight downturn, but it quickly recovered and moved on to new heights. The period was also one of increased commercial and business activity. Of forty-four Utah firms listed in Hogle's handbook in 1917, twelve of the twenty-nine for which dates of incorporation were given were organized after 1910.[56] In manufacturing, farming, transportation, and mining, Utah's economy experienced an upward trend during the nine years. Working conditions had never been better, and the people of Utah enjoyed higher wages and better lives. The legislature passed laws providing better conditions for women and children, for the regulation of utilities and banks, and for workmen's compensation.

Still, as the next essay explains, a combination of factors prevented Utah from passing the threshold into an urban-industrial economy. It seems probable that the orderly character of economic growth in Utah was disrupted by wartime developments. Resources were pressed by expanded markets into marginally productive agricultural, mining, and manufacturing enterprises—enterprises which undoubtedly would not have been undertaken in the absence of wartime prices and markets. This development had disastrous results for the state's economy after the wartime boom had subsided.

3. The Economic Consequences of the War: Utah and the Depression of the Early 1920s

Thomas G. Alexander

Economic historians have generally seen the depression of 1921 as a temporary dislocation. Most have agreed that agriculture suffered during the 1920s, but this decline has generally been viewed as an aberration.[1] But for Utah and probably for the other mountain western states as well, the depression was not merely temporary. The expansion of the economy which accompanied World War I brought about excessively rapid capital formation, reallocation of resources, and high employment in agriculture, mining, and manufacturing. After the war, however, markets could not be found for goods produced by states suffering the disadvantages of geographic isolation and relatively low population. The depression of the early 1920s exposed the economy of Utah to competition not felt during wartime, revealing the tenuous nature of markets upon which the recent flush of prosperity had been built. Although construction, railroading, and trade continued to sustain the economy, the further shocks of 1929 opened these businesses as well to renewed pressure. The depression of the early 1920s was a part of the price Utahns paid for shifting resources to marginal mining, manufacturing, and agricultural enterprises during the war.

Between 1910 and 1920 Utah's economy grew like a crop of wild morning glory in July. Employment in manufacturing increased at a faster rate than that of either the United States or the Mountain West. Although the state ended the decade less industrialized than the United States average, it was (by percentage of employees in manufacturing) the most industrialized state in the Mountain West, and prospects for the future seemed promising. Capital invested in manufacturing increased from $47 million to $131 million between 1909 and 1919. This was a 175 percent increase, substantially greater than the 144 percent increase for the nation as a whole.[2]

The manufacture of beets into sugar, together with the primary processing of other products of Utah's fields and mines, underpinned Utah's industrial growth. By December 1919 Ogden had become one of the ten leading grain-milling centers of the United States, and the Salt Lake Valley had developed a smelter district with a composite copper, silver, and lead production greater than any other district in North America. Mills and smelters refined ores from Utah and parts of Idaho, Nevada, Montana, and Arizona. A small chemical industry had developed on the by-products of this processing. A tentative entry into iron and steel manufacturing was begun at Midvale, south of Salt Lake City.[3]

In spite of a brief dislocation caused by the beginning of the First World War in Europe, mining moved to new heights. Although the number of mines decreased from 675 to 202, the aggregate capital invested in Utah mines increased 81 percent, from $98 million to $187 million between 1909 and 1919. The percentage of the whole working force employed in mining declined somewhat, but the number so employed increased slightly. Copper production increased from 109 million pounds in 1909 to 246 million pounds in 1917. Beginning in 1915, the Tintic district southwest of Provo entered what some observers thought was the greatest period of prosperity in its history. The annual value of the product of Utah mines doubled during the decade, coal production reached record levels, and potash deposits on the Great Salt Lake and near Marysvale in south-central Utah were developed.[4]

Agriculture, which was Utah's foremost employer, showed increases even more spectacular than those in manufacturing or mining. While agricultural employment in the United States declined, Utah's agricultural force increased both absolutely and relatively (see table 3.1). New lands were opened in outlying regions of Utah, increasing agricultural acreage from 3.4 million

TABLE 3.1
Aggregate Capital and Capital per Acre of Utah Farms, 1880-1940

	Capital on Farms in Millions of $ (Land, Buildings, Implements, and Livestock)	Capital per Acre	Percentage Increase or Decrease	Acres in Farms (Millions)
1880	$ 19.3	$27.60	.....	.7
1890	39.5	30.30	.....	1.3
1900	75.2	18.30	.....	4.1
1910	150.8	45.50	.....	3.4
1920	311.0	62.20	+36	5.0
1925	250.0	50.00	- 19	5.0
1930	286.3	52.90	+ 4	5.6
1940	198.5	27.20	- 49	7.3

SOURCE: Computed from University of Utah Bureau of Economic and Business Research, "Measures of Economic Changes in Utah," *Utah Economic and Business Review* 7 (December 1947).

to 5.0 million. Aggregate capital invested in agriculture grew more than 100 percent, from $151 million to $311 million. Of particular importance was the development of Utah's beet sugar industry. Utah moved to third place among the states in beet sugar production, as under the stimulus of wartime need the price of beets increased from seven dollars per ton in 1917 to twelve dollars per ton in 1920.[5]

Other businesses shared in this prosperity. The Eccles, Bamberger, and Orem interurban electric railways stretched from Payson on the south to Preston, Idaho, on the north, and narrow-gauge steam railways spread into the mining districts. After its incorporation from a number of smaller utilities in 1912, the Utah Power and Light Company expanded its power network to include communities from Ashton, Idaho, on the north to Huntington, Utah, 370 miles to the south. Assets of Utah banks increased from $752,000 in 1910 to $1,255,000 in 1920. Between 1900 and 1920 per capita income in Utah increased from $183 to $556—a jump of 203 percent. This was only slightly less than the increase in the United States as a whole.[6]

Utahns seemed to believe that this rapid growth would continue. In January 1917, shortly before America's entry into World War I, Utah Governor Simon Bamberger assured his constituents that

> *while a portion of the stimulus may have been provided by the European war, the continuance of that war is in no wise essential to the continued prosperity of the state. Competent authorities hold that the present high price of metals will be maintained irrespective of the course of the warring powers. While food products may decrease slightly in price, the Utah farmer will not lose much, for he is learning by scientific intensive farming to produce a larger crop per acre each year and with an established market his future is assured.*[7]

Not again until predictions by economists of a "permanently high plateau" in 1929 were "competent authorities" more wrong.[8] With the end of the war, Utah's economy entered into a depression which toppled agriculture, mining, and manufacturing from their pinnacle. Although mining and agriculture paced the decline, various components of the Utah business community languished to one degree or another from 1919 through 1922.

Mining Distress

The depression had its earliest impact on the mining industry (see fig. 3.1). After peaking in 1917, mineral prices generally lagged behind those of consumer goods. The unsatisfactory price levels of 1919 placed minerals in the vanguard of depressed business. In 1919 the total output of gold, silver, copper, lead, and zinc dropped 54 percent below the 1918 level. By 1920 copper production had declined to 116 million pounds from a 1917 high of 246 million. In 1921 the output of all metals decreased 96 percent in volume and 56 percent in value

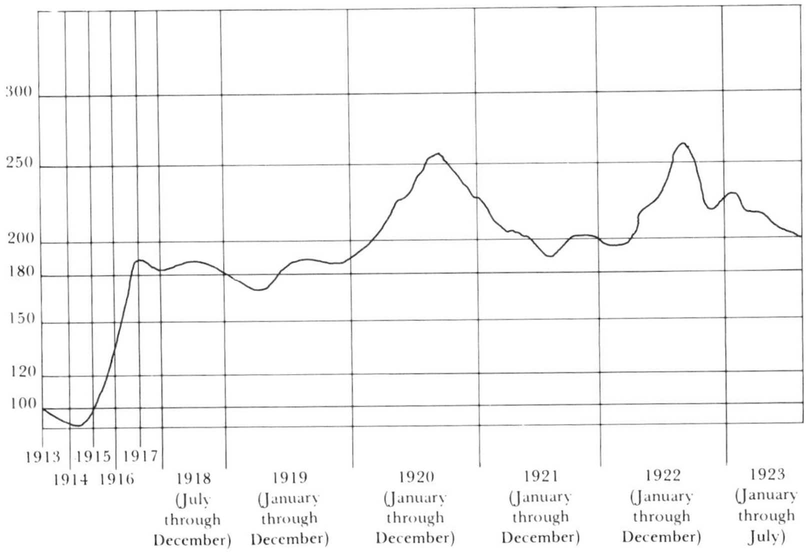

Fig. 3.1. Bureau of Labor Statistics Index of Wholesale Mineral Product Prices, 1913-23 (1913=100). Data from *Federal Reserve Bulletin* 8 (September 1922) and 9 (July and December 1923).

below the 1920 level. In 1919 only eleven companies—about half the number of 1918—paid dividends; the same number paid dividends in 1921.[9]

Even industrial giants like the Utah Copper Company suffered from declining markets. In 1918 its earnings had been $11.60 per share. In 1919 they declined to $5.08, and in 1920 they were only $3.03. In 1920 the company maintained a $6.00-per-share dividend by dipping into cash reserves, but by 1921 the dividend had fallen to only $2.50 per share. Utah Copper was one of the few companies to pay a dividend that year. On March 29, 1921, seven of the largest copper companies in the United States ceased operations, and several others stopped in April. Utah Copper's Magna flotation plant had shut down on February 26, 1919, and the Arthur concentrator and Garfield smelter closed in April 1921. Utah Copper did not reopen its operations until April 2, 1922. Even then, the company operated at a net deficit of more than $100,000 for the second quarter of 1922. That was a decided improvement, however, from the $1.3 million deficit during the same quarter a year before.[10]

Distress in other sectors of the mining industry was generally not as severe or long lasting as in copper. The repurchase provisions of the Pitman Silver Act of 1918 assisted the silver, lead, and zinc industries. Even with that support, the price of silver began to decline in the spring of 1920. The impact on some Tintic mines like the Eureka Lilly Mining Company was severe, and in late December 1920 the company announced suspension of operations because of its inability to discharge indebtedness. The response of many mines in the Tintic district and at Park City, however, was to increase production in 1920 over 1919. Tintic increased its output from 6,921 carloads of ore in 1919 to 7,397 carloads in 1920, and Park City removed 75,623 tons of ore in 1919 and 99,864 in 1920. Still the *Salt Lake Tribune* reported early in 1921 that the past year had been the most "trying that the mines of this [Tintic] district have weathered through a great many years." Mines in the Tintic district continued to break records for production during the first half of 1921, even though earnings declined. In the third quarter of 1921 Tintic Standard declared no dividend, in the fall of 1921 most of the mines closed, and by the end of the year all major lead and copper companies were either idle or doing only maintenance work.[11]

Early in 1922, however, conditions began to improve. Employment increased during May, but dividends for all Utah mines were actually lower during the first half of 1922 than for the same period in 1921. Only in districts like Tintic and Park City, where silver and lead were the main products, were dividends higher, probably because of federal price support for silver.[12]

Coal mining was the one major sector of Utah's mining industry which suffered even less than silver-lead mining between 1919 and 1922. As late as May 1921 the Federal Reserve Board pointed out that the price of bituminous coal, unlike many prices, remained 100 percent above pre-1914 levels. Nevertheless, declining demand forced Utah mines to curtail production during the first half of 1921. By June the volume of production had declined to less than half that of 1920, and the mines ended the year with production about 77 percent of the 1920 figure.[13]

Several minor industries in Utah were also damaged by the depression and other sources of instability. By the early 1920s Utah had developed a small but thriving oil industry. Nevertheless, by the end of 1921 reports indicated that the industry was still on unsure ground and that the economic dislocations of the year had damaged prospects for a healthy survival. All but twelve of 128 potash companies in Utah had failed by 1922 due to the reopening of shipping lanes from Europe and the reorganization of the international potash cartel. By 1926 five more Utah companies had been eliminated.[14]

Nevertheless, by the end of 1922 most of Utah's mineral industry appears to have been back on its feet. Production was high for the remainder of the decade, and profits seem to have followed (see table 3.2). Still the recovery was uneven. Employment in all the mineral industries declined over the decade (see fig. 3.2), and the price of some products such as coal declined as well. There appears also to have been a net decline in capital—probably owing to a decline in the value of plants and equipment. On balance, it might be said that mining at best had reached a plateau.[15] (See table 3.3 for assessed valuation of mining property, as well as of railroads and agricultural property, from 1915 to 1930.)

Agricultural Decline

If mining suffered the initial shock, it was agriculture which suffered the greatest long-term distress from the depression. Throughout the years from 1896 to 1914, wheat at a dollar a bushel had been a major goal. By 1922, however, as the *Salt Lake Tribune* put it, dollar wheat was no longer a goal but a dreaded disaster. Whereas wheat had sold in 1919 for between $3.35 and $3.50 per bushel, by November 1921 it had dropped to ninety-eight cents.[16]

TABLE 3.2
Production and Value of Utah Mines, 1916-30

	Approximate Value of Aggregate Capital (Millions of $)	Value of Product (Millions of $)	Value of Product as Percentage of Aggregate Capital
1916	......	$ 99.7	..
1917	......	113.6	..
1918	......	105.8	..
1919	$187.0	64.2	34
1920	205.7	76.5	37
1921	225.0	40.6	18
1922	215.1	60.7	28
1923	213.4	86.2	40
1924	204.6	84.4	41
1925	202.4	100.3	49
1926	198.0	99.0	50
1927	207.4	90.4	43
1928	202.4	97.4	48
1929	201.3	115.1	57
1930	211.2	64.2	30

SOURCE: Aggregate capital of Utah mines for 1919 is from U.S. Bureau of the Census, *Fourteenth Census of the United States Taken in the Year 1920,* vol. 11: *Mines and Quarries, 1919* (Washington, D.C., 1922). Aggregate capital for the years 1920 through 1930 is computed from table 3.3 under the assumption that the value of the capital would bear approximately the same relationship to the assessed valuation of the capital in the other years as it did in 1919. In 1916 the legislature ordered the county assessors and the State Board of Equalization and Assessment to assess all property at its market value in accordance with a provision of the state constitution. This was clearly not done, but the assumption that a fairly constant relationship remained between the two variables seems warranted. Unfortunately, 1919 was the last year in which the Census Bureau estimated aggregate capital. It estimated aggregate capital in 1909, but before 1919 the method of reporting assessments makes impossible the computation of the value of the capital for comparison. Value of the product is from U.S. Geological Survey, *Mineral Resources of the United States,* 1916 through 1923, and U.S. Bureau of Mines, *Mineral Resources of the United States,* 1924 through 1930.

TABLE 3.3

Assessed Valuation of Utah Property, 1915-32

(in Millions of Current Dollars)

	Assessed Valuation	Agricultural Property		Mining Property				Railroads
		Land	Livestock	Real Estate		Improvements and Machinery	Claims	Land and Improvements
1915	$227.9	$ 32.7	$11.6	.....	$ 4.1	.....	$2.1	$31.7
1916	531.9	87.3	28.2	.....	8.3	.....	2.7	72.6
1917	593.0	92.1	33.1	.....	9.7	.....	2.8	74.8
1918	677.2	98.4	47.2	.....	11.4	.....	2.4	80.7
1919	692.5	114.1	42.6	$10.2		$22.9	.58	92.8
1920	716.9	133.1	34.2	13.5		23.1	.79	96.0
1921	687.8	133.4	23.5	14.8		25.3	.77	96.8
1922	635.5	115.4	22.2	14.0		24.5	.61	94.8
1923	646.7	108.9	24.7	13.6		24.0	.63	94.4
1924	665.5	100.4	23.9	11.6		24.9	.67	95.7
1925	668.6	99.5	24.2	11.5		24.6	.71	93.8
1926	696.1	101.5	25.7	11.2		24.1	.72	93.1
1927	701.8	101.9	25.5	12.3		24.7	.74	92.8
1928	700.7	100.8	28.5	11.8		24.2	.76	93.7
1929	723.1	100.8	27.5	11.5		24.4	.74	94.9
1930	728.4	99.1	22.4	11.4		26.2	.75	95.4

SOURCE: *Biennial Reports of the State Board of Equalization and Assessment,* 1915 through 1929, and *Biennial Reports of the Utah State Tax Commission,* 1931 and 1932.

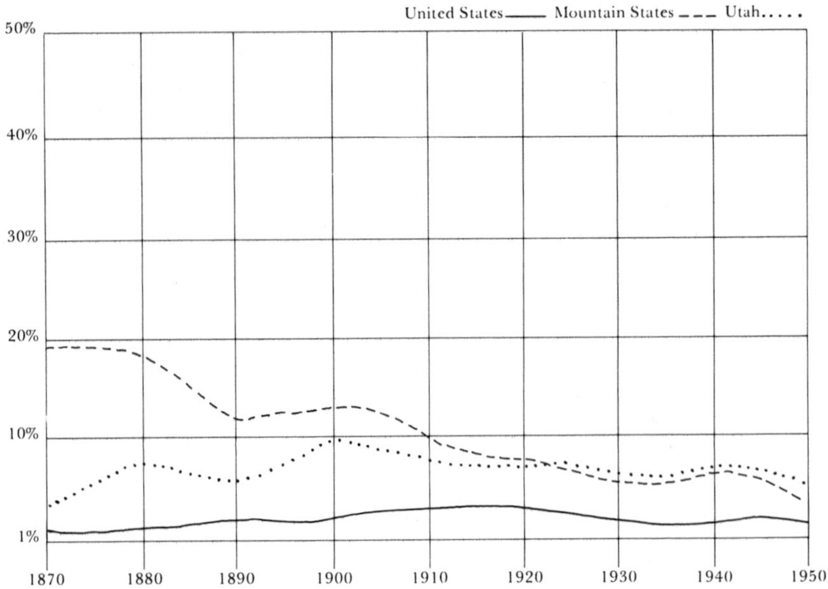

Fig. 3.2. Percentage of the Labor Force Employed in Mining, 1870-1950. Data from Leonard J. Arrington, *The Changing Economic Structure of the Mountain West,* 1850-1950, Utah State University Monograph Series, vol. 10, no. 3 (Logan, June 1963).

Until October 1920 the price levels for most agricultural commodities had stood above prices farmers paid for most other goods. The price of eggs in Utah, for instance, rose from $6.00 per case in 1917 to $24.50 in December 1920. During the same period, the price of whole milk increased from sixteen cents per gallon to twenty-seven cents.[17]

During the winter of 1920-21, agricultural prices declined precipitately (see figures 3.3 and 3.4), and farmers began to hold back the sale of storable crops. By May 1921 reports from the Twelfth Federal Reserve District indicated that the price of wool, lambs, barley, and wheat had declined to about the 1913-14 level, and the price of cattle stood even lower. At the same time, the general price level for consumer goods remained

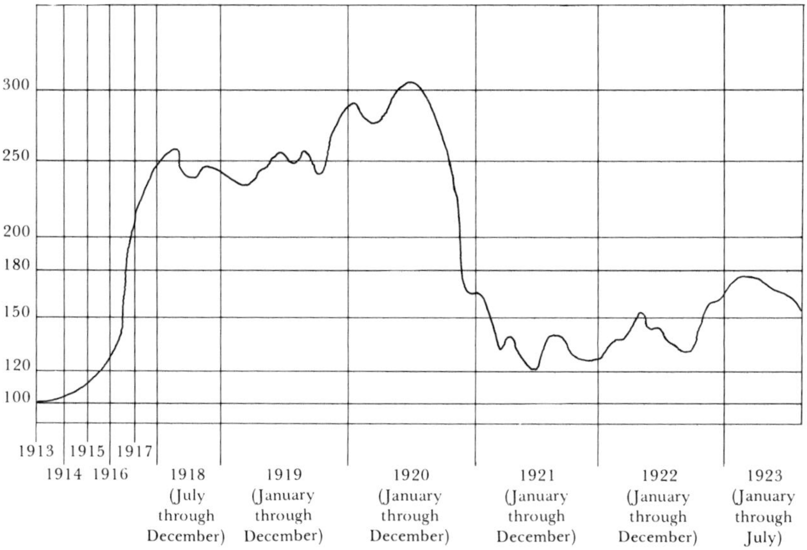

Fig. 3.3. Bureau of Labor Statistics Index of Wholesale Crop Product Prices, 1913-23 (1913=100). Data from *Federal Reserve Bulletin* 8 and 9.

50 percent above that of 1913. In March 1921 it was estimated that 35 percent of Utah's previous year's wheat crop and 20 percent of the corn crop were still on the farms. Inventories of cheese, meat, fish, eggs, and fruits began to build up in cold storage.[18]

Distress came even earlier for wool growers and cattlemen than for crop farmers. Utah ranked fourth among the states in wool production, and as the price of wool declined in 1919, growers found it necessary to withhold wool from the market in the hope of a price rise. By the end of 1920 distress was widespread, and some observers believed that only the mild winter of 1920-21 saved a number of stockmen from ruin by allowing them to cut operating costs.[19]

Payments to sugar beet farmers underwent a similar decline. Beet prices dropped from $12.03 per ton in 1920 to $5.47 per ton in 1921, which was the lowest price between 1916 and

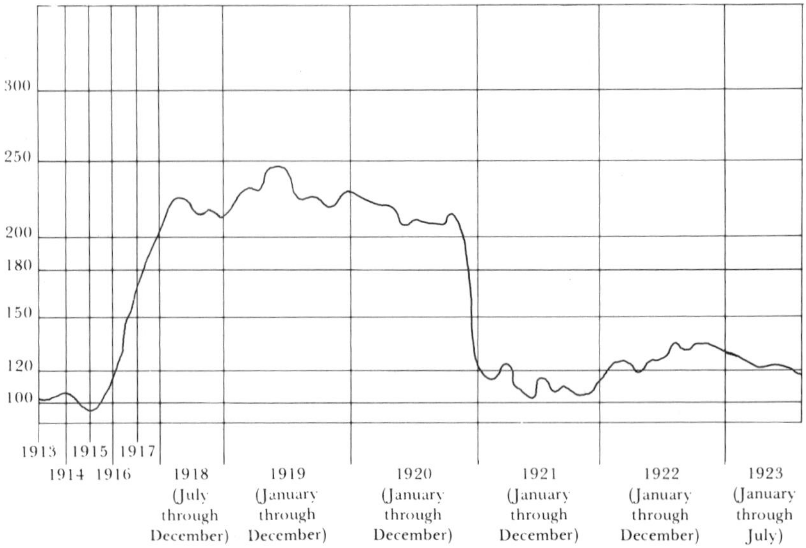

Fig. 3.4. Bureau of Labor Statistics Index of Wholesale Animal Product Prices, 1913-23 (1913=100). Data from *Federal Reserve Bulletin* 8 and 9.

1932. Utah farmers received about $3 million for beets in 1921, about half the amount they had earned a year earlier. In 1922 beet farmers left the business in droves, and the acreage of beets in Cache Valley was about 60 percent of the 1921 level.[20]

By mid-1922 agricultural prices seemed to be stabilizing, but as harvests began in the late summer, profits declined even more. Grain prices equaled the lows of 1921, and the value of a number of commodities—including corn, oats, barley, eggs, chickens, and peaches—were actually below 1921 levels. The State Board of Agriculture reported that the prices had been the "discouraging feature of the season." Some apples and potatoes were not even harvested because prices were too low to pay for transportation to markets. Fortunately for stockmen, sheep and lamb prices were considered "satisfactory," and cattle prices improved slightly.[21]

These low prices were compounded in the late summer and

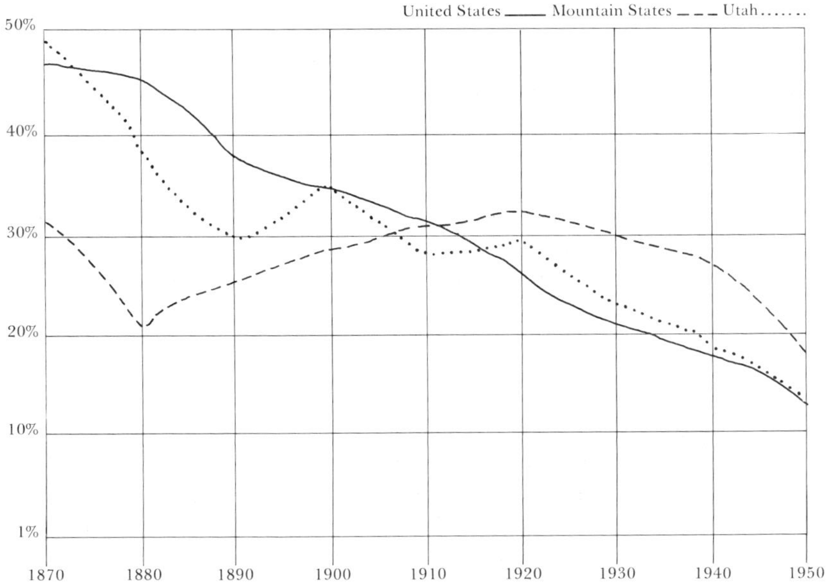

Fig. 3.5. Percentage of the Labor Force Employed in Agriculture, 1870-1950. Data from Arrington, *Changing Economic Structure.*

early fall of 1922 by a railroad shopmen's strike which added a shortage of railroad cars to the farmer's bag of woes. On August 18, both the Utah Farm Bureau Federation and a delegation of Brigham City peach farmers pled with President Harding to intervene in the strike. The labor dispute was not promptly settled, however, and reports indicated that part of the fruit crop—about 20 percent in Utah County, for instance—was lost.[22]

In the years after 1922 agricultural conditions continued to remain unsatisfactory (see fig. 3.5). Prices in 1923 were still called "discouragingly low," and in 1924 the Utah State Industrial Commission reported considerable discontent over prices. Even more serious for the future of Utah agriculture was the fact that capital invested in farms began to decline in absolute and relative amounts. During the 1920s Utah agriculture actually became less capital-intensive, as the amount of capital per acre declined 19 percent, from $62.20 in 1920 to $50.00 in 1925. By contrast, capital per acre had increased 36 percent during the preceding decade. Reports of the State Board of Equalization indicate a large percentage of this decline came in the value of land which had been purchased at inflated wartime values.[23] This represented, then, actual capital losses which could be recovered only through increased profits or higher land values, neither of which was available to Utah farmers until the Second World War.

Manufacturing Cutbacks

The effect of the 1920s depression on manufacturing more nearly paralleled its effect on mining than on agriculture. By 1919 Utah had developed more than one thousand manufacturing establishments employing nearly nineteen thousand men. By 1921 the number of businesses declined to 645 and employment dropped to 13,300. After the depression, however, both employment and value added by manufacture seemed to have reached a plateau. The largest reduction in employment came in food processing, which declined from just under two thousand employees in 1919 to slightly more than one thousand in 1929. Increases in employment in textile production and furniture manufacture could not offset the declines.[24]

Illustrative of the distress of manufacturing is the example of beet sugar processing. The disastrous drop in sugar prices which followed the implementation of the Underwood-Simmons Tariff in 1913 was followed by new markets and sugar scarcity after the opening of World War I in 1914. The value of Utah-Idaho Sugar Company stock rose from seven dollars per share in 1914 to twenty-nine dollars in 1916, and the company opened new factories in Spanish Fork, West Jordan, Layton, and Brigham City. Other companies opened plants at Moroni, Delta, and Springville. During the war, controls allowed the price of sugar to rise only from 7.25¢ to 9.00¢ per pound, but afterward the lifting of regulation allowed a rise to 23.57¢ in May 1920. Then, as European sugar began to reach the American market, the price broke and tumbled to 1.81¢ per pound by the end of 1921.[25]

During the expansion of the previous decade, the Utah-Idaho Sugar and the Amalgamated Sugar companies had followed the practice of mines and farms by converting liquid assets into capital. As the market broke they began to borrow to meet payments to beet producers. Financing was extremely difficult to secure, and U and I Sugar was forced to reduce its nominal capitalization and replace its top management in order to borrow from Bankers Trust Co. of New York. Amalgamated reported a loss of more than $5 million in 1920, and cuts in beet production forced it to close its Logan plant for the 1922 season. Amalgamated paid no dividends from 1918 to 1930, and U and I Sugar lost money every year between 1925 and 1930.[26]

Other sectors of the food processing industry were badly hurt as well. Governor Charles R. Mabey and his family had invested heavily in a canning plant at Woods Cross during World War I. During the war the federal government had stockpiled much of the pack, and after the armistice Washington began dumping cases of canned goods on the market. In his reminiscences, Mabey attributed the depressed market of the early twenties to this governmental action. It seems probable that the causes were more complex, but it is clear that policies of the government bear some responsibility.[27]

Fluctuations in metal prices were mirrored in the operation of the metal processing plants. Various Utah Copper Company operations closed, and the Magna flotation plant did not reopen until November 11, 1922, after having been closed for 3½ years. Most operations at the International Mining, Smelting, and Refining Company plant at Tooele remained closed during all of 1921, although the lead furnaces continued to operate until July 5. On April 19, 1922, the International smelter began to employ men for repair work. Ore was then being shipped to the smelter, and operations had resumed at the company's Ophir Hill concentrator. The Utah Steel Company plant at Midvale, however, closed never to reopen.

One bright spot in Utah's manufacturing picture in the 1920s

TABLE 3.4
Commercial and Industrial Failures, 1918-34

	Utah				Mountain States				United States			
	No. of failures	Rank	Current liability ($1000)	Rank	No. of failures	Rank	Current liability ($1000)	Rank	No. of failures	Rank	Current liability ($1000)	Rank
1918	85	13-14	410	16-17	410	14	2,975	16	9,982	15	163,020	16
1919	67	16	723	15	271	16	2,416	17	6,451	17	113,291	17
1920	81	15	1,632	8	315	15	5,785	14	8,881	16	295,122	14
1921	85	13-14	1,333	10	714	8	14,427	6	19,652	12	627,402	4
1922	148	4	2,129	6	845	2	15,063	3	23,676	5	623,896	5
1923	124	8	4,109	3	737	5	14,862	4	18,718	13	539,387	7
1924	118	10	2,324	4	729	6	10,417	8	20,615	10	543,225	6
1925	140	5	1,128	12	727	7	10,886	7	21,214	9	443,744	12
1926	155	2	1,700	7	777	3	8,438	9	21,773	8	409,232	13
1927	137	6	1,168	11	617	11	7,903	12	23,146	6	520,104	8
1928	103	12	915	14	584	13	6,855	13	23,842	4	489,560	10
1929	113	11	1,568	9	596	12	8,057	11	22,909	7	483,250	11
1930	129	7	4,691	2	709	9	16,084	2	26,355	3	668,284	3
1931	149	3	2,212	5	764	4	14,747	5	28,288	2	736,309	2
1932	206	1	4,903	1	910	1	17,033	1	31,822	1	928,313	1
1933	121	9	937	13	633	10	8,329	10	20,307	11	502,831	9
1934	59	17	410	16-17	251	17	3,153	15	12,185	14	204,218	15

SOURCE: University of Utah Bureau of Economic and Business Research, "Measures of Economic Changes in Utah, 1847-1947," *Utah Economic and Business Review* 7 (December 1947).

was Columbia Steel Company's development of a pig iron plant at Ironton, between Provo and Springville. The company constructed short railroads to bring together coal from Carbon County and iron from Iron County. Production began in October 1923, and between May 1924, when the first iron flowed, and December 1931 the company produced 1.8 million tons of coke and 1.0 million tons of iron. Most of the iron went to California for further processing, but some businesses using iron for pipe and other products established themselves near the plant. The company also used coke to produce by-products such as coal tar, ammonium sulphate, and benzol.[28]

Still, the disaster to Utah's economy caused by the depression of the early 1920s was not offset by these successes. The aggregate current liability of businesses which failed in Utah during the four years from 1921 through 1924 was actually greater than the liability of failures from 1931 through 1934 (see table 3.4).[29] Thereafter, neither employment (see fig. 3.6) nor value added by manufacture grew in any consistent way during the remainder of the decade.

One sector of Utah's economy which seems not to have suffered permanent damage from the depression was Utah's transportation industry. Employment in railroading increased from 7,700 in 1920 to 8,000 in 1930. Contemporary reports indicate that, although the railroads had to reduce freight rates and employment and revenues declined during 1921, the impact of the depression was not severe. In July 1921, for instance, the Union Pacific actually increased its labor force by one thousand men. In fact, the bitter shopmen's strike of 1922 seems to have hurt railroading more than the depression (see fig. 3.7). Outside of railroading, firms such as Pacific Intermountain Express and Interstate Motor Lines began the development of a Utah-based, long-range trucking industry in the late twenties.[30]

In spite of the health of the railroads, Utah's isolation from competing water transportation put the state at a disadvantage in seeking national markets for its shattered economy. During the First World War, water transportation to the Pacific Coast had been curtailed, and freight rates posed no particular obstacle to Utah business. As a result, Utahns developed markets

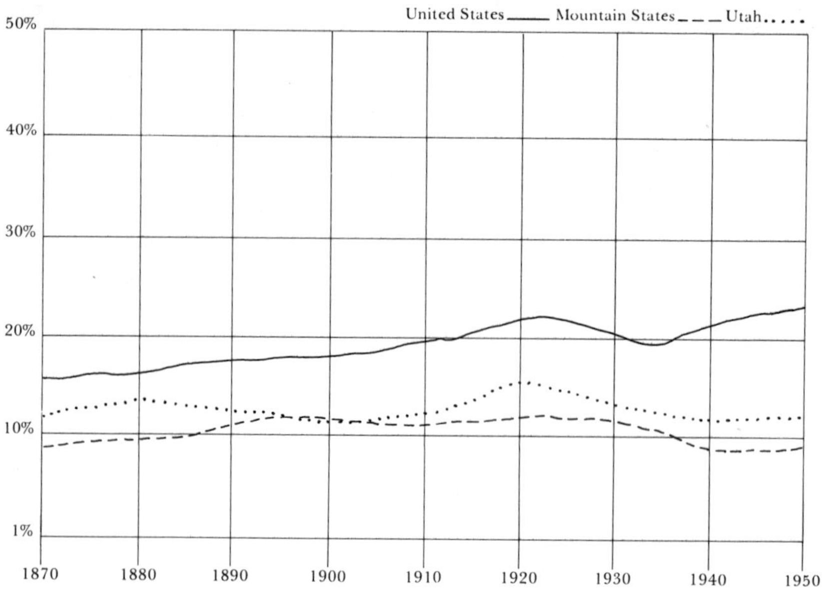

Fig. 3.6. Percentage of the Labor Force Employed in Manufacturing, 1870-1950. Data from Arrington, *Changing Economic Structure.*

which could not be maintained after the reopening of normal water routes. A combination of rail and water transportation put eastern and midwestern cities at an advantage in west coast markets. Freight rates gave Utah an advantage in the Denver market, but it enjoyed no such access east of the hundredth meridian. Governor Charles R. Mabey wrote to Secretary of Commerce Herbert Hoover in an attempt to get freight rates reduced, and Utah's Senior Senator Reed Smoot worked to strengthen the power of the Interstate Commerce Commission. Neither effort had much effect.[31]

Utah's problems were compounded by the basing point system used in the steel industry. In July 1924 the Federal Trade Commission ordered United States Steel to cease and desist from the practice, but the system remained in effect until July 1948, when the steel industry adopted an FOB mill

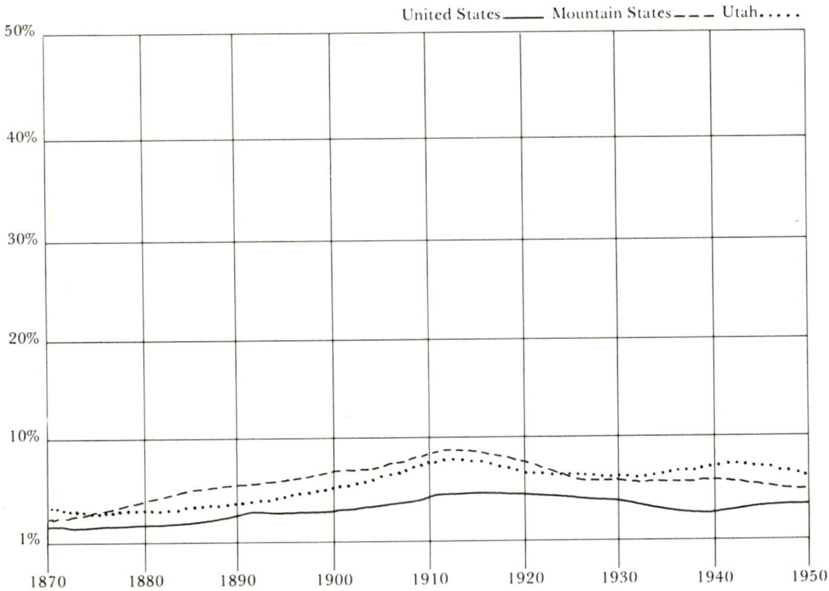

Fig. 3.7. Percentage of the Labor Force Employed in Railroading, 1870-1950. Data from Arrington, *Changing Economic Structure*.

basis.[32] Because Utah has successfully developed a steel industry employing five thousand men since World War II, it is entirely possible that its earlier steel industry might have been able to expand rather than close had freight rates been more favorable in the 1920s.

Unlike mining or agriculture, retail trade did not begin to suffer until 1921 (see table 3.5). Zion's Cooperative Mercantile Institution of Salt Lake City reported that in 1920 it transacted the largest volume of business of any year in its history to that time. January 1921 was the first month during the depression when the volume of retail sales was less than that of the corresponding month in the previous year. Sales during 1922, however, continued to suffer and averaged below the 1935-39 level. Prices declined, and the cost of sirloin steak in Salt Lake City in July 1921 stood at 30.8¢ per pound, which was lower than in

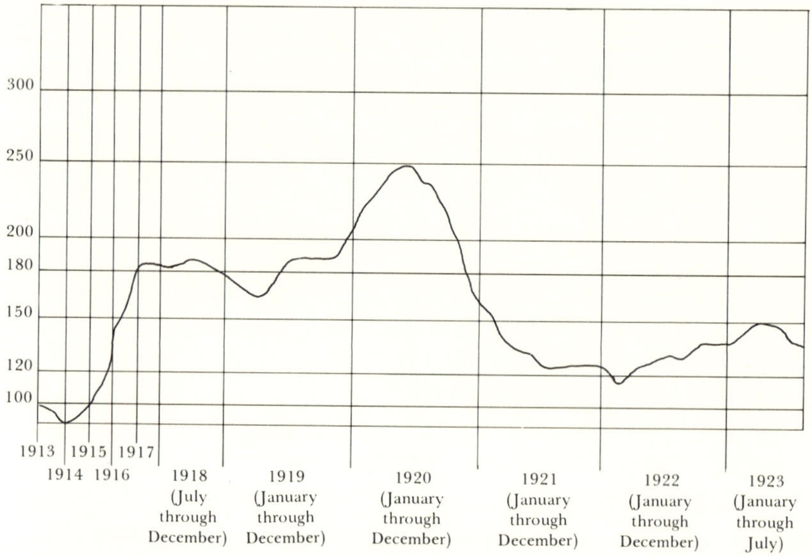

Fig. 3.8. Bureau of Labor Statistics Index of Wholesale Producers' Goods Prices, 1913-23 (1913=100). Data from *Federal Reserve Bulletin* 8 and 9.

any other major city in the United States except Portland, Oregon, and was twelve cents lower than the price in July 1913. By October 1921 it was reported that prices in Salt Lake City had declined to about the 1912 level.[33] (See figures 3.8 and 3.9 for 1913-23 wholesale producers' and consumers' goods prices.)

By late 1922 retail sales began to increase. They did not reach the 1920 level in most Utah areas until 1925 and not until 1926 in Salt Lake City. One of the factors in recovery was apparently the demand for automobiles, which was reportedly high as early as April 1922.[34]

In spite of the relatively high price of building materials and high interest rates, the volume of new construction was hardly affected by the depression. Apparently the demand for buildings, which had developed because of shortages during World War I, had grown to such an extent that construction was demanded in spite of the cost. In 1920 the value of building con-

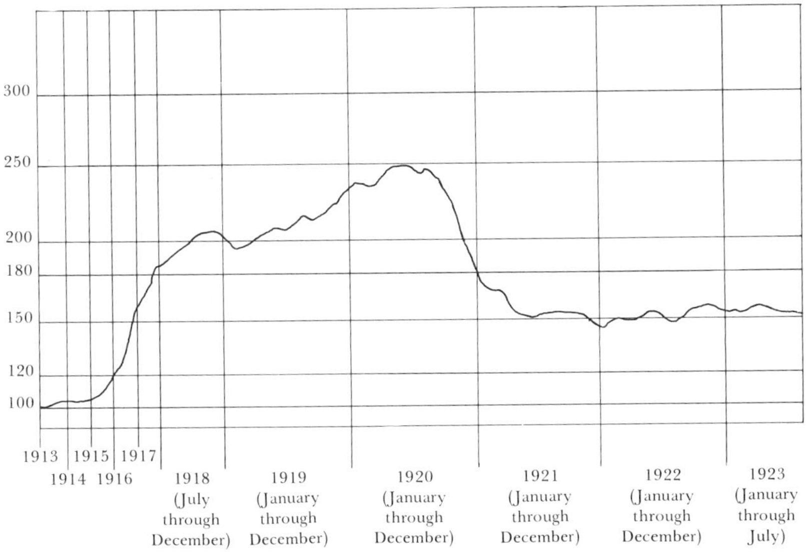

Fig. 3.9. Bureau of Labor Statistics Index of Wholesale Consumers' Goods Prices, 1913-23 (1913=100). Data from *Federal Reserve Bulletin* 8 and 9.

struction in Salt Lake City was only slightly lower than in 1919 ($3.84 million as compared with $4.06 million). A high volume of construction continued through 1921, and the Federal Reserve Board noted that this trend, which was contrary to that of the nation as a whole, was characteristic of the Far West. In March 1921 Salt Lake City issued building permits for $250,583 worth of construction as compared with $166,460 in the same month in 1920.[35]

The boom in construction continued throughout 1921 and into 1922, and it appears that residential housing paced other types of construction. The value of permits in May 1921 was more than double the value for May 1920, and the volume seemed to increase monthly. In August 1921 the value was 152 percent higher than August 1920; in October, 284 percent higher than October 1920; and in November, 430 percent higher than November 1920. Beyond the residential construc-

TABLE 3.5
Net Retail Sales in Salt Lake City and the Twelfth Federal Reserve District, 1918-22
(Comparison of percentage of increase or decrease in net retail sales with the corresponding month of the previous year)

	1919					1920						
	Aug	Sep	Oct	Nov	Dec	Jan	Feb	Mar	Apr	May	June	July
SLC	+23.2	+33.4	+44.8	+42.7	+32.3	+23.8	+11.5	+10.5	+ 7.1	+26.4	+18.3	+20.6
12th	+20.3	+40.6	+82.0	+46.1	+50.7	+51.7	+31.1	+37.8	+13.8	+31.2	+27.8	+21.2
	1920					1921						
	Aug	Sep	Oct	Nov	Dec	Jan	Feb	Mar	Apr	May	June	July
SLC	+11.6	. . . .	+ 8.9	+14.7	+ 9.1	- 0.6	- 5.2	+ 1.7	- 8.7	-18.7	- 6.1	-16.2
12th	+21.7	+14.5	+ 8.2	+11.3	- 4.3	-14.3	- 2.4	+ 0.6	- 9.3	- 4.1	- 7.8	-12.9
	1921					1922						
	Aug	Sep	Oct	Nov	Dec	Jan	Feb	Mar	Apr	May	June	July
SLC	-15.3	-13.9	-20.9	-14.2	-16.0	-19.9	-22.1	-20.7	- 9.0	- 3.3	- 5.5	- 5.6
12th	- 6.2	- 8.7	- 6.3	- 7.9	- 3.0	- 6.3	- 9.1	- 6.2	- 1.3	+15.1	+ 3.0	+ 3.1
	1922											
	Aug	Sep	Oct	Nov	Dec							
SLC	+ 0.2	- 0.4	+ 7.2	+ 2.1	+ 4.2							
12th	+ 5.7	+ 3.7	+10.3	+12.0	+14.5							

SOURCE: *Federal Reserve Bulletin*

tion, work on projects like the Ogden Arsenal, the Scofield Reservoir, the Salt Lake Federal Reserve Branch Bank, and the Bamberger and Orem interurban railways helped keep this industry active.[36]

Banking and Governmental Influences on the Economy

The stress placed upon Utah's economy by the depression, together with ill-advised federal reserve monetary policies, unquestionably damaged Utah's banking community. Probably in response to erratic policies of the board and increasing distress in Utah mining and agriculture, the discount rate on prime commercial paper in Salt Lake City's open market declined from a high of 6 percent in November 1918 to a low of 5 percent in February 1919. In July it began to rise. It reached 6 percent in December 1919, jumped to 7 percent in March 1920, and to 8¼ percent in September. Its next low was 7½ percent in April 1921, when quotations for that category of discount were ended for the remainder of the depression.[37]

The Utah banking community shared with banks in the United States as a whole the problem of a great many small units in small towns which were unable to weather the stress of financial conditions in the 1920s. The number of banks in the state reached an all-time high of 134 in 1920 and declined every year of the 1920s except 1924, when the number of new banks equaled the number of failures. While the number of banks decreased, the assets of the largest banks climbed. Thus, in spite of the bank failures, assets of Utah banks increased from $1.26 million in 1920 to $1.9 million in 1930.[38]

As the economy experienced reverses, the state and local governments of Utah also suffered. Assessed valuation of Utah property reached a peak of $717 million in 1921, then began to decline. Much of the reduction came about as marginal agricultural property, which had been purchased during and immediately after World War I, fell in value. State income taxes on metal mines also declined. In order to try to make ends meet, the state government began to cut expenditures and terminate employees. In June 1920, 440 employees had worked in state

TABLE 3.6
Disbursements for Principal Purposes by Utah State Government, 1919-24 (in Millions for Fiscal Years Ending November 30)

	Education	Highways	Debt retirement and service
1919	$5.086	$6.274	$1.272
1920	3.787	7.357	1.028
1921	3.426	7.831	3.570
1922	5.079	5.136	1.020
1923	5.341	5.341	1.436
1924	6.365	5.688	2.053

SOURCE: State of Utah, *Biennial Reports of the Auditor of the State of Utah,* 1919-20 and 1921-22.

offices; in June 1921, that number had been reduced to 380.[39]

In fact, the state government appears to have followed a rather contradictory policy during the depression (see table 3.6 and fig. 3.10). While calling for the reduction of local expenditures and attempting to promote economy on the state level, Governor Charles R. Mabey urged local governments and the federal government to respond to the needs of the people by providing relief and employment. While the state was running a budgetary deficit, the State Land Board made loans to farmers, and the state promoted an extensive highway construction program partly with federal highway funds.[40]

Public school districts and local governments were also subjected to contradictory pressures during 1921 and 1922. In June 1922 State Superintendent of Public Instruction C. N. Jensen reported that all districts showed a 10-12 percent reduction from 1921 budget levels. This was achieved by reducing salaries, calling a moratorium on merit increases, and cutting the school year. Nevertheless, total 1922 school expenditures exceeded 1921 expenses because of expansion in the high schools and colleges. County officials reduced the number of employees and cut salaries. Still, commitments for highway construction

Fig. 3.10. Income and Disbursements of Utah State Government, 1909-24 (in millions of dollars). Data from *Biennial Report of the Auditor of the State of Utah 1919-20, 1921-22, and 1923-24.*

made extensive budget constriction impossible. In spite of opposition from the Chamber of Commerce and the Utah Manufacturers Association, Ogden and Salt Lake City inaugurated some special public works projects to ease unemployment. Salt Lake City also opened a free employment service which doubled as a relief agency by distributing fish and potatoes to the needy.[41] However unintentional and inadequate they may have been, deficit expenditures between 1919 and 1922 undoubtedly helped Utah citizens weather a serious economic problem.

Still, these efforts were not enough to relieve the distress. Deputations of the unemployed pressed local and state officials to do more. Private relief agencies and charities came to the assistance of many, and public officials urged children to drink more milk and exhorted housewives to hire the unemployed to do their spring cleaning. Salt Lake banks voted to subscribe $60,000 for stock in a foreign trade financing corporation in the hope of stimulating further employment, and many companies went on short shifts to try to spread the work around.[42]

Aside from these state, local, and private activities, the federal government undertook a number of programs to assist in relief. The Harding administration revived the War Finance Corporation to give emergency loans to sugar producers and stockmen. These loans helped some producers, but others complained that these measures were not broad enough. Borrowers could not secure loans by wool or dairy cattle—only by land, sheep, or beef cattle. Also, Utah Senators Reed Smoot and William H. King and Congressmen Don Colton and Elmer Leatherwood attempted to get the federal government to undertake a broader range of public works projects such as new public buildings, expansion of reclamation projects, and changes in the minerals leasing act to promote further employment.[43]

As a supplement to these short-term measures, the protective tariff was expected to provide long-term assistance. Although Woodrow Wilson had vetoed emergency tariff support for agriculture in 1920, the Republican-controlled Congress pushed through a similar act in May 1921. This act protected only agricultural commodities, but the Fordney-McCumber Act of September 1922 extended and broadened protection of agriculture and minerals while placing agricultural implements and breeding animals on the free list.[44]

Critics of these measures have argued that the tariff proved ineffective in protecting agriculture because there was little expansion of the production of such commodities as sugar and wool and because it raised prices to consumers. That a tariff increases prices is clear, but the tariff is a subsidy, and one person's benefit is another's expense. The condition of both agriculture and mining in the 1920s made some sort of subsidization necessary to promote stability. Whether the tariff was the best way to do it is open to question, but it is specious to argue against a subsidy simply because someone must pay the bill.[45]

The argument that the tariff was ineffective simply because agriculture and mining failed to expand rapidly during the 1920s neglects to consider the severity of the condition of these two industries. It is clear that a tariff could not assist farmers of wheat and corn, but any commodity for which domestic consumption was greater than or equal to domestic production could have been subsidized to some degree by the tariff. Among commodities most important to Utah's economy, the domestic consumption of sugar, beef, mutton, wool, and copper all exceeded domestic production each year from 1921 through 1924. Even for these items, the rapid expansion of agriculture during World War I and the violent depression afterwards made continued expansion too much to expect without the provision of a subsidy which probably would have resulted in the production far exceeding the consumption. Certainly the experience of agriculture following World War II ought to demonstrate that any attempt to promote continued expansion during a time of excessive production cannot solve such problems. All the tariff could provide was temporary stability, and then only for businesses not already producing beyond the capacity of consumers to purchase at existing income levels. Some contemporary observers believed that the tariff had helped the prices for wool and sheep.[46]

Working against the positive effects of these measures were a number of ill-considered federal activities and policies. In May 1919 the federal government announced abandonment of most wartime business controls. This action undoubtedly contributed to the inflation which followed. In addition, the Federal Reserve Board was so concerned with financing federal debt operations that it allowed the discount rate to remain at 4¾ percent until January 1920, when it announced an abrupt increase to 6 percent. This policy of loose money followed by stringent contraction probably contributed to the increase in the prime commercial rate of Salt Lake City's banks from 6 percent to 7 percent and to the continuing increase during 1920, while Utah's economy plummeted from its peak prosperity.[47]

Labor Disputes

If certain federal policies hurt Utah businesses, the attitude of state officials and prominent citizens was antithetical to the interests of Utah laborers. Business gained after 1921 from efforts to improve economic conditions, but labor lost virtually all it had won in the previous twenty years. During the period after 1900, strong union organization and a high degree of job control—if not characteristic of Utah's mining camps—were at least major features of skilled occupations in Salt Lake City and Ogden. After 1919 economic distress, fear of radical revolution, antiforeign hysteria, and antiunion sentiment virtually killed Utah's labor movement.[48]

Workers themselves were partly responsible for the response of the community to the maintenance of strong union organization. In February 1919 laboring men in Salt Lake County organized a Workers', Soldiers', and Sailors' Council on the Soviet model, and the Salt Lake Federation of Labor, by a vote of sixty-seven to five, endorsed the Russian revolution and the overthrow of all exploiting classes. In the state Federation of Labor convention in September, radicals won further endorsement of their aims, and M. P. Bales, a Salt Lake barber who was shortly to become a member of the Communist Party, became president of the Utah State Federation of Labor. During the depression Bales was a leader of the Council of Unemployed, which worked against the efforts of the Chamber of Commerce and Utah State Manufacturers Association and in favor of public works and better conditions for the unemployed.[49]

In perspective, however, the radicalism of 1919 was short lived since businessmen and conservative workers staged a counterrevolution which broke the back of Utah's labor movement. Already in 1918 a group of businessmen and civic leaders had organized the Utah Associated Industries with the avowed purpose of ending labor disputes and establishing the open shop throughout Utah. In early 1920 the Associated Industries moved to break the union movement in the construction trades, and by mid-1921 they achieved a partial open shop and wage reductions. Possibly the most vigorous battle developed between the employers' organization and the typographical union. Although the conflict raged for 3½ years, by September 1924 the union capitulated. Ironically, this union had been the most conservative in the state and had earlier formed a bulwark against radical unionism. By the late 1920s the Utah Federation of Labor became little more than a name, its newspaper folded in 1924, and at the annual convention in 1929 only fifteen delegates representing seven unions—most of them from Ogden—even bothered to attend.[50]

The business community had emerged victorious. Among other things, it had succeeded in securing legislation prohibiting peaceful picketing and outlawing any interference with the importation of strikebreakers. At its annual banquet in November 1927 the Utah Associated Industries hosted Governor George H. Dern, President Heber J. Grant of The Church of Jesus Christ of Latter-day Saints, and Monsignor Duane G. Hunt, Rector of the Catholic Church's Cathedral of the Madeleine, who was the principal speaker. In a circular sent out in May 1928 the Utah Associated Industries Organization boasted that it had restored industrial peace and freedom in 1920 and that since that time labor unions had been unable to "retrieve their lost power." It went on to warn that no

> *contractor, builder, employer or employee should be engaged to do any kind of work unless he actually operates the open shop. Nothing should be done that will encourage, abet or assist those who are planning this renewal of oppression.*[51]

The organization's letterhead indicated that a broad range of business, religious, and civic leaders supported the movement. John G. M. Barnes, former president of the Utah Bankers Association, was president; and Charles W. Nibley, second counselor in the First Presidency of the LDS Church, and Marriner S. Eccles, of the First Security Banking Corporation and later of the Treasury Department and Federal Reserve Board, were among the vice-presidents.

Given the condition of Utah's economy and the increasing intransigence of businessmen, it is not at all surprising that labor disputes, wage cuts, and unemployment characterized the years from 1919 through 1922. As early as February 1919 the Twelfth Federal Reserve District reported increasing unemployment in Utah, and by March joblessness affected about five thousand workers—mostly miners and the unskilled. Unemployment continued at abnormally high levels through 1920; by June 1921 the U.S. Employment Service reported the improbability of any "improvement until the mining depression is relieved." By April 1922, however, the reopening of copper operations, announcements of new construction, and improved agricultural prices presaged increased employment. By October 1922 labor shortages were actually reported in some areas, particularly construction, coal mining, and retail trade.[52]

A Period of Economic Depression

Thus did Utah pay a heavy price for America's crusade to make the world safe for democracy. For more than three years—early 1919 to mid-1922—the economy of the state had been wracked by economic disturbances from which it did not fully recover until after the 1930s. The value of the product of the mining industry did not reach the average of 1916 through 1918 until 1929 and then not again until 1941. Agriculture had been dealt a blow from which it was not to recover until World War II, and manufacturing had not recovered by 1950. In fact, when measured by percentage of the work force employed, Utah was actually more industrialized in 1920 than in 1950. Utah's labor movement had been shattered, and a community antagonism developed which has continued to recent years. The relative vigor of construction, transportation, and trade do not appear to have offset these losses, and Utah showed a net population outflow in each census through 1940.[53]

Some of the problems of Utah's economy seem to have been shared by other mountain western states. Undoubtedly the greatest damage was done to agriculture, which was then the largest single source of employment in the region. Markets opened by wartime conditions stimulated the reallocation of resources, particularly in increased investment and employment. Every mountain western state except Nevada had an absolute increase in agricultural employment during the decade between 1910 and 1920, and all except New Mexico and Wyoming, two of the most agricultural states, experienced percentage increases as well. This trend was contrary to that of the United States, which was becoming less, rather than more, agricultural. Under the pressure of high prices, marginal and submarginal land was opened, and capital was invested which could not earn adequate returns during the 1920s. As a result, agricultural employment declined.[54]

These capital losses were compounded by ecological destruction. As land which had been broken for valuable crops such as sugar beets was abandoned, Russian thistle, wild mustard, shadscales, and saltbrushes replaced native grasses. These weeds served as breeding places for beet leafhoppers, which transmitted the curly-top virus to beet fields. Competition from abroad together with natural destruction forced the closing of a number of beet sugar plants in Utah and other states.[55]

The long-range damage to Utah and mountain western manufacturing, although very severe, is probably less apparent and is obvious only in comparison with the impact of World War II on the region's economy and the results of California development. Aggregate capital invested in manufacturing in the Mountain West increased more than three times, from $213 million in 1909 to $751 million in 1919. During the same period industrial capital in California increased at a lower rate, from $483 million to $1,139 million. Nevertheless, the Pacific Coast crossed the "threshold of urban-industrial society"—a step which the Mountain West could not make. As a result, employment in manufacturing in the three most industrialized states of the Mountain West—Utah, Colorado, and Montana—declined between 1920 and 1930.[56] As with agriculture, rapid capital formation in industry had produced excess capacity as mountain western businessmen were unable to find markets to absorb their products. Adverse freight rates, the decline of markets for food products, the lack of expansion of markets for processed minerals, and relatively small population in the Mountain West itself contributed to this situation.[57]

Healthy sectors of the economy (such as construction, railroading, and trade) seem to have sustained the economy of the Mountain West over the plateau created by adversity in agriculture, mining, and manufacturing.[58] These businesses could probably have continued to serve as the basis for further economic growth had consumers continued the demand for their products. After 1929 such markets were unavailable, and the plateau which these industries helped to sustain crumbled under the pressure of basic structural weakness.

If one phenomenon was responsible more than any other for the condition of the economy of Utah and the Mountain West during the 1920s, it was the misallocation of resources wrought by the expansion that had been stimulated by World War I. By creating markets for manufactures, agricultural products, and minerals, wartime demand moved resources into fields of activity which could not be sustained after the armistice. By the same token, wartime shortages created temporary demands for consumer products and residential construction. After the war, manufacturers, farmers, and miners in other parts of the country and abroad were in a more favorable position to meet the demand for goods. Opportunities for gainful employment in Utah declined, and net population outflow resulted. Despite the responsibility of national policy for the dislocations, lack of concern by the Wilson administration failed to prevent the damage, and the Harding administration's measures were tardy and inadequate.

Ironically, the condition of Utah and the Mountain West in the early 1970s does not hold out promise of avoiding a repetition of the experience of the 1920s. Should expenditures for the Department of Defense be cut severely and tourism under the pressure of current oil shortages be curtailed, the region's economy undoubtedly would be badly shocked. Manufacturing which is closely tied to fluctuations in government contracts would be severely hurt, and federal employment, which enjoys the status of a basic industry in the region, would be curtailed.

Under this situation—unless the federal government undertook measures to relieve the distress—agriculture, transportation, and mining (including oil operations) would have to sustain the economy of the region. If the experience of the 1920s and the recent experience of Seattle are any criteria of the concern of the federal government for distress caused by its policies, Utah and the Mountain West cannot be entirely hopeful. Conceivably the region could suffer again the economic consequences of depending on a capricious defense-stimulated demand for its products.

The basic question raised by this essay is not whether the movement to an urban-industrial economy would have been possible or even desirable for Utah, but rather whether orderly and gradual development is preferable to major, rapid shifts of resources under the stimulation of forces such as war contracts and other massive short-term programs. If Utah's development is any criterion, the answer seems to be that massive infusions of capital and shifts in resources, while temporarily beneficial, may bring about a misallocation of resources which, when the immediate stimulus is removed, are difficult to move into other areas. The effect of such erratic patterns of development has been especially severe in agriculture, at least until the recent growth of agribusinesses, because families have been unequipped to foresee long-term trends and have poured their savings and lives into the development of farms which could not compete during postwar and postinfusion times. In manufacturing, mining, or any other economic activity so stimulated, the invested resources may be difficult to reallocate, particularly if they are in areas isolated from the markets where their products may be sold.

Notes

Chapter 1

The writer is grateful for a grant from the Utah State University Research Council which made possible the research on which this study was based.

1. "Minutes of the First Presidency and Quorum of the Twelve, Journal History of the Church," 27 January 1898, Archives Division, Historical Department, The Church of Jesus Christ of Latter-day Saints, Salt Lake City.

2. The opening of the mines in the 1870s altered, but did not transform, Utah society. Economically, the miners opened up pockets of wealth which were shipped out of the state without a fundamental change in the structure of the economy.

3. Cited in Clark C. Spence, *British Investments and the American Mining Frontier, 1860-1901* (Ithaca, 1958), p. 109.

4. Leonard J. Arrington, *Great Basin Kingdom: An Economic History of the Latter-day Saints, 1830-1900* (Cambridge, Mass., 1958), pp. 383-84.

5. It is to be noted that the basic data for 1900 is not identical with that given by Easterlin in Conference on Research in Income and Wealth, National Bureau of Economic Research, *Trends in the American Economy in the Nineteenth Century* (Princeton, 1960), 24:104.

6. See Leonard J. Arrington, "The Mormon Tithing House: A Frontier Business Institution," *Business History Review* 28 (March 1954): 29. Approaching this problem from a different angle, Easterlin estimates the 1900 agricultural service income per worker in Utah at $285. Assuming that Cache Valley obtained its income almost exclusively from agriculture

and that some persons in the community, particularly non-Mormons, contributed nothing, and ruling out the children who paid only nominal tithing, one might easily arrive at the $285 figure. Indeed, the writer had estimated Cache Valley average income at around $200 in the 1880-1910 period. Joel E. Ricks, ed., and Everett L. Cooley, assoc. ed., *The History of a Valley: Cache Valley, Utah-Idaho* (Logan, 1956), p. 238.

7. Leonard J. Arrington, *The Changing Economic Structure of the Mountain West, 1850-1950,* Utah State University Monograph Series, vol. 10, no. 3 (Logan, June 1963), p. 63.

8. Wain Sutton, ed., *Utah: A Centennial History,* 3 vols. (New York, 1949), 1:167.

9. *Deseret News,* 14 December 1907, p. 30.

10. Sutton, 1:153, 209.

11. Leonard J. Arrington, "The Deseret Agricultural and Manufacturing Society in Pioneer Utah," *Utah Historical Quarterly* 24 (April 1956): 165-70.

12. Alvin Johnson, *Pioneers' Progress* (Lincoln, Nebr., 1960), p. 293.

13. Sutton, 1:307.

14. See annual editions of the *Salt Lake Tribune* and *Deseret News* for the years 1905 to 1910; see also U.S. Bureau of Reclamation, *Reclamation Project Data* (Washington, 1961), pp. 728-33.

15. This is based upon Douglas D. Alder, "The Ghost of Mercur," *Utah Historical Quarterly* 29 (January 1961): 35-41.

16. Adapted from Leonard J. Arrington and Gary B. Hansen, *"The Richest Hole on Earth": A History of the Bingham Copper Mine,* Utah State University Monograph Series, vol. 11, no. 1 (Logan, October 1963), pp. 15-66.

17. Harvey J. O'Connor, *The Guggenheims: The Making of an American Dynasty* (New York, 1937), p. 290.

18. *Salt Lake Tribune,* 30 December 1906, p. 83.

19. What follows is based upon Thomas G. Alexander, "From Dearth to Deluge: Utah's Coal Industry," *Utah Historical Quarterly* 31 (Summer 1963): 237-41.

20. Helen Zeese Papanikolas, "The Greeks of Carbon County," *Utah Historical Quarterly* 22 (April 1954): 145-47.

21. Don Sorensen, "Wonder Mineral: Utah's Uranium," *Utah Historical Quarterly* 31 (Summer 1963): 282-85.

22. *Deseret News,* 21 December 1901, p. 1, part 6.

23. See Osmond L. Harline, "Utah's Black Gold: The Petroleum Industry," *Utah Historical Quarterly 31* (Summer 1963): 291-311.

24. *Salt Lake Tribune,* 1 January 1899, p. 50.

25. Ibid., 3 January 1909, p. 6.

26. *Salt Lake Tribune,* 20 December 1900, p. 20; *Great Basin Kingdom.* pp. 391-93.

27. *Great Basin Kingdom,* pp. 386-91; *Salt Lake Tribune,* 1 January 1905, p. 80, and 2 January 1910, p. 33.

28. *Salt Lake Tribune,* 2 January 1910, p. 48.

29. *Great Basin Kingdom,* pp. 308-9.

30. Ibid., pp. 394-99.

31. Sutton, 2:828.

32. *Salt Lake Tribune,* 1 January 1898, p. 3.

33. Roland Stucki, *Commercial Banking in Utah, 1847-1966* (Salt Lake City: University of Utah College of Business, 1967).

Chapter 2

1. Harvey S. Perloff, Edgar S. Dunn, Jr., Eric E. Lampart, and Richard F. Muth, *Regions, Resources, and Economic Growth* (Baltimore, 1960), p. 190.

2. J. R. Mahoney, "Measure of Economic Changes in Utah, 1847-1947," *Utah Economic and Business Review* 7 (December 1947):13, 46, 48.

3. Arvil L. Stark, "History of Growing Fruit in Utah," in *Utah: A Centennial History,* ed. Wain Sutton, 3 vols. (New York, 1949), 1:113 ff.

4. George Stewart, "History of Varieties of Field Crops in Utah," in Sutton, 1:105-8.

5. F. S. Harris, "The Agriculture of Utah," *Utah Agricultural Experiment Station Circular No. 44* (Logan, April 1921), pp. 8, 19.

6. Mahoney, p. 11; personal interview with Lee Walker, whose father homesteaded on the reservation in 1915 (Provo, Summer 1965).

7. 35 *U.S. Statutes at Large,* 639; 37 *U.S. Statutes at Large,* 123; and 39 *U.S. Statutes at Large* 639. See also Lawrence B. Lee, "The Homestead Act: Vision and Reality," *Utah Historical Quarterly* 30 (Summer 1964): 234.

8. J. A. Hogle & Co., *Hand Book of Utah Securities: Industrial, Banking, and Financial, 1917* (Salt Lake City, 1917), pp. 15-19; E. B. Brossard, "Some Types of Irrigation Farming in Utah," *Utah Agricultural Experiment Station Bulletin No. 177* (Logan, December 1920), p. 40.

9. The following is based on Brossard, pp. 5-6, 10-11, 15-18. Average farm size in 1910 was 156.7 acres and in 1920 was 196.8 acres. Tenancy in 1910 stood at 7.9 percent and in 1920 at 10.9 percent. Full ownership was 79.3 percent in 1910 and 74.5 percent in 1920. Mahoney, pp. 46, 48. On improvement in the dairy herds see State of Utah, *Report of the Industrial Commission of Utah, Period July 1, 1917-June 30, 1918,* pp. 163-66.

10. Brossard, p. 37.

11. Brossard, pp. 30, 36; Harris, p. 19; Mahoney, p. 11; and Gertrude M. McCheyne, "Rural Conditions in the State of Utah," in State of Utah, *Report of the Industrial Commission, 1917-18,* p. 198.

12. The following is based upon Thomas G. Alexander, "Utah's First Reclamation Project: The Strawberry Valley Project," *Utah Historical Quarterly.* For a discussion of other reclamation projects see State of Utah, *First Biennial Report of the State Bureau of Immigration, Labor, and Statistics for the Years 1911-1912,* pp. 40-43.

13. "Utah's Roseate Future," *New West Magazine* 7 (December 1916): 14; F. S. Harris and N. I. Butt, "Sugar-Beet Production in Utah," *Utah Agricultural College Experiment Station Circular No. 34* (Logan, December 1918), pp. 26-28; State of Utah, *Report of the Industrial Commission, 1917-18,* p. 177; and Alfred G. Rees, "Utah Industrially," *Utah Educational Review* 13 (May-June 1920): 351.

14. Morris E. Garnsey, *America's New Frontier: The Mountain West* (New York, 1950), p. 108.

15. State of Utah, *Report of the Industrial Commission, 1917-18,* pp. 177-79.

16. State of Utah, *Report of the Bureau of Immigration, Labor, and Statistics, 1915-16,* p. 236; Elroy Nelson, *Utah's Economic Patterns* (Salt Lake City, 1956), p. 40; and Fred G. Taylor, "Notes on the Development of the Beet Sugar Industry in Utah," in Sutton, 2:939-40.

17. "Utah's Roseate Future," p. 14; Utah-Idaho Sugar Company, *Twenty-Fifth Annual Statement, 29 February 1916.*

18. *Between the Millstones: The Arguments to the Jury in the Utah-Idaho Sugar Beet Case (The People Are the Jury)* (Salt Lake City, 1918), p. i; Isaac Russell, "The Corporate Vulture Flock," *Progressive* 1 (8 March 1913): 10-11; and Charles Nibley, "Statement to the Stockholders of the Utah-Idaho Sugar Company," *New West Magazine* 11 (July 1920): 58-59.

19. Nelson, p. 52; State of Utah, *Report of the Bureau of Immigration, Labor, and Statistics, 1915-16,* p. 241; and ibid., 1913-14, p. 248.

20. "Ogden Meats for Allies," *New West Magazine* 8 (September 1917): 27-32; State of Utah, *Report of the Bureau of Immigration, Labor, and Statistics, 1915-16,* pp. 241-43; and "Utah's Roseate Future," p. 16.

21. "Raising Livestock in Utah," *New West Magazine* 8 (December 1917): 29-30; S. S. Jensen, "Livestock and Packing Industry," *Proceedings of the Tenth Annual Convention of the Utah Bankers Association* (Logan, 1918), pp. 98-102.

22. State of Utah, *Report of the Bureau of Immigration, Labor, and Statistics, 1915-16,* p. 241; W. E. Zupann, "Ogden—Western Livestock Center," *New West Magazine* 10 (December 1919): 5-8.

23. State of Utah, *Report of the Industrial Commission, 1917-18,* pp. 167-68; O. J. Stillwell, "Ogden a Grain Milling Center," *New West Magazine* 10 (December 1919): 10-12.

24. State of Utah, *Report of the Bureau of Immigration, Labor, and Statistics, 1913-14,* pp. 236-47; idem, *Report of the Industrial Commission, 1917-18,* pp. 156-57; and "Ogden Helping Hoover," *New West Magazine* 8 (September 1917): 18-21.

25. State of Utah, *Report of the Industrial Commission, 1917-18,* pp. 168-71; idem, *Report of the Bureau of Immigration, Labor, and Statistics, 1915-16,* p. 253.

26. State of Utah, *Report of the Bureau of Immigration, Labor, and Statistics, 1915-16,* p. 241; idem, *Report of the Industrial Commission, 1917-18,* p. 152; and Rees, "Utah Industrially," p. 351.

27. State of Utah, *Report of the Industrial Commission, 1917-18,* pp. 175-76.

28. Sunset Magazine Homeseekers' Bureau of Information, *Salt Lake City and the State of Utah* (n.p., [ca. 1912]), p. 26; Nelson, p. 113; Gustive O. Larson, "Bulwark of the Kingdom: Utah's Iron and Steel Industry," *Utah Historical Quarterly* 31 (Summer 1963): 255; "Utah's Roseate Future," p. 13; and State of Utah, *Report of the Industrial Commission, 1917-18,* pp. 152, 184.

29. State of Utah, *Report of the Bureau of Immigration, Labor, and Statistics, 1915-16,* pp. 248-50.

30. Leonard J. Arrington and Gary B. Hansen, *"The Richest Hole on Earth": A History of the Bingham Copper Mine,* Utah State University Monograph Series, vol. 11, no. 1 (Logan, October 1963), p. 84; *Salt Lake City and the State of Utah,* p. 24; D. A. Lyon, R. H. Bradford, S. S. Arentz, O. C. Ralston, and C. L. Larson, *Metallurgical Treatment of the Low-Grade and Complex Ores of Utah: A Preliminary Report,* Bureau of Mines Technical Paper 90 (Washington, D.C., 1915), p. 9; United States Geological Survey, *Mineral Resources of the United States, Calendar Year, 1912,* 2 vols. (Washington, 1913), 1:883. Hereafter these volumes will be cited as *Mineral Resources* with the year and volume.

31. *Mineral Resources* (1911), 1:752; ibid., (1912), 1:890-91; ibid., (1913), 1:375-80; ibid., (1915), 1:393; ibid., (1919), 1:426; and Thomas Varley, C. C. Stevenson, and W. Spencer Reid, *Utah's Mineral Wealth Represented by Statistics and Graphic Charts Compiled from Official Government and State Reports* (Salt Lake City, 1921), p. 28.

32. Nelson, p. 170; Arrington and Hansen, p. 74.

33. Leonard J. Arrington, *The Changing Economic Structure of the Mountain West, 1850-1950,* Utah State University Monograph Series, vol. 10, no. 3 (Logan, June 1963), pp. 34-35, 45-46.

34. Arrington and Hansen, pp. 57, 68-70; Elroy Nelson, "The Mineral

Industry: A Foundation of Utah's Economy," *Utah Historical Quarterly* 31 (Summer 1963): 184; B. S. Butler, G. F. Loughlin, V. C. Heikes, et al., "The Ore Deposits of Utah," United States Geological Survey Professional Paper 111 (Washington, 1920), pp. 120, 129-31; *Mineral Resources* (1912), 1:882-83; ibid., (1914), 1:725; ibid., (1915), 1:393; ibid., (1917), 1:176; and ibid., (1918), 1:373.

35. Mahoney, pp. 68-69; Butler, pp. 133-35, 142; Varley, pp. 14, 17 ff.; G. W. Crane and Howard Fitch, eds., *The Tintic Mining District of Utah: Prepared for the Tintic Meeting of the Utah Section of the American Institute of Mining Engineers, July 15, 1915* (n.p., 1915), pp. 14-25; "Memorial from the Rocky Mountain Lead-Ore Producers to the Sixty-Third Congress of the United States, Special Session" (Salt Lake City, 1913); and Bert B. Brewster, "A Brief History of Mining in Utah," in Sutton, 2:892.

36. Brewster in Sutton, 2:888; Butler, pp. 132-33; and *Mineral Resources* (1912), 1:885. For an extended discussion of conditions at Mercur, see Douglas D. Alder, "The Ghost of Mercur," *Utah Historical Quarterly* 29 (January 1961): 33-42.

37. *Mineral Resources* (1911), 2:932; State of Utah, *Report of the Industrial Commission, 1915-16*, pp. 251-52; ibid., 1917-18, pp. 174-75; *Mineral Resources* (1917), 2:240-41; and Miles P. Romney, "Utah's Cinderella Minerals: The Nonmetallics," *Utah Historical Quarterly* 31 (Summer 1963): 234.

38. State of Utah, *Report of the Industrial Commission, 1917-18*, pp. 174-75; Nelson, *Utah's Economic Patterns*, p. 173; *Mineral Resources* (1917), 2:413; Romney, "Cinderella Minerals," p. 231; B. S. Butler and H. S. Gale, "Alunite: A Newly Discovered Deposit Near Marysvale, Utah," in *United States Geological Survey Bulletin 511* (Washington, n.d.), pp. 5-6.

39. Thomas G. Alexander, "From Dearth to Deluge: Utah's Coal Industry," *Utah Historical Quarterly* 31 (Summer 1963): 237-40.

40. Noble Warrum, *Utah Since Statehood: Historical and Biographical*, 4 vols. (Chicago, 1919), 1:311; State of Utah, *Report of the Bank Commissioner for the Period Commencing April 1, 1921, to and Including November 20, 1922*, p. 3; and John G. M. Barnes, "Annual Address of the President," in *Proceedings of the Tenth Annual Convention of the Utah Bankers Association* (Logan, 1918), p. 20.

41. Nelson, *Utah's Economic Patterns*, p. 274; Warrum, 1:354; "Ogden's Largest Industry," *New West Magazine* 8 (September 1917): 22; "Utah's

Roseate Future," p. 17; *Mineral Resources* (1910), 1:580; ibid., (1912), 1:891; and Butler, *Ore Deposits*, pp. 119-20.

42. Garnsey, p. 185; Jensen, "Packing Industry," in *Proceedings of Convention of Utah Bankers*, pp. 102-3; Rees, "Utah Industrially," pp. 349-51.

43. Sutton, 2:985, 991; Nelson, *Utah's Economic Patterns*, p. 262.

44. Utah Power and Light Company, *Electrifying the Wheels of Progress 1912-1922* (n.p., [ca. 1922]), pp. 2-14; Brewster in Sutton, 2:891.

45. Mahoney, pp. 10, 13.

46. Dale L. Morgan, "The Changing Face of Salt Lake City," in *The Valley of the Great Salt Lake*, rev. ed. (Salt Lake City, 1963), p. 27.

47. Everett L. Cooley, "Utah's Capitols," ibid., pp. 73-85.

48. For a general discussion of Progressivism on the national level, see George Mowry, *The Era of Theodore Roosevelt and the Birth of Modern America, 1900-1912* (New York, 1958) and Arthur S. Link, *Woodrow Wilson and the Progressive Era, 1910-1917* (New York, 1954). Unless otherwise indicated, the discussion on progressive legislation is taken from the various reports of the Utah State Bureau of Immigration, Labor, and Statistics and the Industrial Commission; Warrum, *Utah Since Statehood; The Compiled Laws of Utah, 1917;* and Callis Blythe Ahlstrom, "Utah and Colorado During the Reform Era, 1890-1917" (master's thesis, Columbia University, n.d.).

49. John M. Hayes, "The Mining Industry of Utah," *Proceedings of the Eleventh Annual Convention of the Utah Bankers Association* (Salt Lake City, 1919), p. 122.

50. See Sutton, 2:1043.

51. Perloff, p. 650.

52. State of Utah, *Report of the Bureau of Immigration, Labor, and Statistics, 1911-12,* p. 29; ibid., 1915-16, pp. 11, 23. Several other businesses, such as the Craig Canning Company, also operated model facilities. See "Women in the Canning Factories," *New West Magazine* 8 (September 1917): 23.

53. State of Utah, *Report of the Bureau of Immigration, Labor, and*

Statistics, 1911-12, pp. 29-30; ibid., 1913-14, p. 15; see also *Mineral Resources* (1912), 1:887 and Frank C. Robertson and Beth Kay Harris, *Boom Towns of the Great Basin* (Denver, 1962), p. 58.

54. State of Utah, *Report of the Bureau of Immigration, Labor, and Statistics, 1911-12,* p. 32; ibid., 1915-16, pp. 16-17; State of Utah, *Report of the Industrial Commission, 1917-18,* pp. 194-95; "Utah's Roseate Future," p. 12.

Chapter 3

The writer expresses appreciation to Wayne Hinton and Michael Cleverley for their assistance with research in the *Salt Lake Tribune,* to Janet Hauck for her help with typing and in the preparation of the charts and tables, and to the Brigham Young University Research Division for financial assistance.

1. George Soule, *Prosperity Decade: From War to Depression, 1917-1929* (New York, 1968), pp. 107, 124-25; John D. Hicks, *Rehearsal for Disaster: The Boom and Collapse of 1919-1920* (Gainesville, Florida, 1961), pp. 32, 86. Unless otherwise indicated, statistical information in this article comes from University of Utah Bureau of Economic and Business Research, "Measures of Economic Changes in Utah," *Utah Economic and Business Review* 7 (December 1947) and Elroy Nelson, *Utah's Economic Patterns* (Salt Lake City, 1956).

2. Everett S. Lee, Ann Ratner Miller, et al., *Population Redistribution and Economic Growth, United States, 1870-1950,* 3 vols. (Philadelphia, 1957-64), 1:697; Leonard J. Arrington, *The Changing Economic Structure of the Mountain West, 1850-1950,* Utah State University Monograph Series, vol. 10, no. 3 (Logan, June 1963), pp. 45-46.

3. O. M. Stilwell, "Ogden a Grain Milling Center," *New West Magazine* 10 (December 1919): 10-12; Thomas Varley, C. C. Stevenson, and W. Spencer Reid, *Utah's Mineral Wealth Represented by Statistics and Graphic Charts, Compiled from Official Government and State Reports* (Salt Lake City, 1921), p. 28; Elroy Nelson, *Utah's Economic Patterns* (Salt Lake City, 1956), pp. 113, 170; Nelson, "The Mineral Industry: A Foundation of Utah's Economy," *Utah Historical Quarterly* 31 (Summer 1963): 185; Leonard J. Arrington and Gary B. Hansen, *"The Richest Hole on Earth": A History of The Bingham Copper Mine* (Logan, 1963), p. 74; State of Utah, *Third Report of the State Bureau of Immigration, Labor, and Statistics, 1915-1916,* pp. 241, 245-48; idem, *Report of the Industrial Commission of Utah, Period July 1, 1917-June 30, 1918,* pp. 152, 171-72, 184; "Utah's Roseate Future," *New West Magazine* 7 (December

1916): 12, 14-15; Alfred C. Rees, "Utah Industrially," *Utah Educational Review* 13 (May-June 1920): 351; and Gustive O. Larson, "Bulwark of the Kingdom: Utah's Iron and Steel Industry," *Utah Historical Quarterly* 31 (Summer 1963): 255.

4. Nelson, "The Mineral Industry," p. 184; "Utah Mines," *Goodwin's Weekly* 26 (1915): 44; U.S. Bureau of the Census, *Thirteenth Census of the United States Taken in the Year 1910,* vol. 11: *Mines and Quarries, 1909,* p. 160; idem, *Fourteenth Census of the United States Taken in the Year 1920,* vol. 11: *Mines and Quarries, 1919,* p. 222; Nelson, *Economic Patterns,* p. 173; U.S. Geological Survey, *Mineral Resources of the United States, 1917,* 2:413; Miles P. Romney, "Utah's Cinderella Minerals: The Nonmetallics," *Utah Historical Quarterly* 31 (Summer 1963): 231; B. S. Butler and H. S. Gale, "Alunite: A Newly Discovered Deposit Near Marysvale, Utah," *U.S. Geological Survey Bulletin 511* (Washington, n.d.), pp. 5-6; and Thomas G. Alexander, "From Dearth to Deluge: Utah's Coal Industry," *Utah Historical Quarterly* 31 (Summer 1963): 237.

5. "Utah's Roseate Future," p. 14; Leonard J. Arrington, *Beet Sugar in the West: A History of the Utah-Idaho Sugar Company, 1891-1966* (Seattle and London, 1966), passim. See table 3.1 and fig. 3.5.

6. Nelson, *Economic Patterns,* p. 274; Utah Power and Light Company, *Electrifying the Wheels of Progress, 1912-1922* (n.p., [ca. 1922]), pp. 2-4; Roland Stucki, *Commercial Banking in Utah, 1847-1966* (Salt Lake City, 1967), pp. 115-16; and Lee et al., *Population Redistribution,* 1:753.

7. Simon Bamberger, "Future Prosperity of Utah," *New West Magazine* 8 (January 1917): 36.

8. See John Kenneth Galbraith, *The Great Crash, 1929* (Boston, 1955), p. 75 and passim.

9. U.S. Geological Survey, *Mineral Resources* (1918), 1:369; ibid., (1919), 1:417, 425; ibid., (1920), 1:285; ibid., (1921), 1:341.

10. *Salt Lake Tribune,* 1 March, 29 April, 9 September, and 8 December 1921, 1 and 2 April and 25 August 1922; Arrington and Hansen, p. 70; and *Mineral Resources* (1921), 1:347.

11. Fred L. Israel, *Nevada's Key Pittman* (Lincoln, 1963), pp. 75-81; *Salt Lake Tribune,* 1, 2, and 16 January, 12 February, 20 March, 3 July, and 21 September 1921; and *Federal Reserve Bulletin* 6 (July 1920): 676.

12. *Salt Lake Tribune,* 19 April, 21 and 27 May, and 9 July 1922; State

of Utah, *Report of the Industrial Commission of Utah, 1920-1922,* pp. 938-39.

13. *Federal Reserve Bulletin* 7 (May 1921): 525; *Salt Lake Tribune,* 8 March, 1 April, and 10 July 1921.

14. *Salt Lake Tribune,* 20 February, 8 May, 3 June, and 18 December 1921; Nelson, *Economic Patterns,* p. 173.

15. See figures 3.1 and 3.2 and table 3.2.

16. *Salt Lake Tribune,* 17 August 1922. See fig. 3.3.

17. State of Utah, *Twelfth Biennial Report of the State Dairy and Food Commissioner of the State of Utah for the Years 1919-1920,* p. 28.

18. State of Utah, *First Biennial Report of the Utah State Board of Agriculture, 1923,* p. 20; *Salt Lake Tribune,* 10 March and 20 June 1921; *Federal Reserve Bulletin* 8 (September 1922): 1093. See figures 3.3, 3.4, and 3.9.

19. *Salt Lake Tribune,* 15 and 20 February and 20 June 1921, *Federal Reserve Bulletin* 6 (January 1920): 26.

20. Arrington, *Beet Sugar,* p. 94; *Salt Lake Tribune,* 16 November 1921, 26 April and 25 August 1922.

21. *Salt Lake Tribune,* 9 April, 21 May, 2, 16, 17, and 31 August, and 29 October 1922; Utah, *Report of the State Board of Agriculture, 1923,* pp. 76-77.

22. *Salt Lake Tribune,* 18 August and 22 September 1922.

23. Utah State University Department of Agricultural Economics, *Utah Agricultural Statistics, 1920-1962* (Logan, 1963), pp. 53-85, 108, 116, 120. See table 3.1.

24. Nelson, *Economic Patterns,* p. 217; U.S. Bureau of the Census, *Fourteenth Census of the United States Taken in the Year 1920,* 11 vols. (Washington, 1923), 11:1486-89; and ibid., *Fifteenth Census, Manufactures, 1929,* 3 vols. (Washington, 1933), 3:301.

25. Arrington, *Beet Sugar,* pp. 79-94.

26. Ibid., pp. 95-97; *Salt Lake Tribune,* 17 September 1921, 26 April and

25 August 1922; and K. A. Moser, "The Beet-Sugar Industry and the Tariff with Special Reference to the Great Basin," (master's thesis, Utah State University, 1933), p. 10.

27. Charles R. Mabey, *Our Father's House: Joseph Thomas Mabey Family History* (Salt Lake City, 1947), p. 219; *Salt Lake Tribune,* 23 March 1921.

28. Alexander J. Gardner, "The Regional Competition of the Iron Industry," (master's thesis, University of Utah, 1932), pp. 32, 36-37, 43-48; *Salt Lake Tribune,* 14 November 1921, 30 June, 8 July, 6 August, and 15 September 1922.

29. See table 3.4.

30. Arrington, *Changing Economic Structure,* pp. 34-35; *Salt Lake Tribune,* 17 February, 12 June, and 17 July 1921; *Poor's Manual of Railroads,* 1922, p. 2082; ibid., 1924, pp. 577-78, 689-90, 2036-37, 2049-50; and Donald Quayle Cannon, "The History of the Trucking Industry in the State of Utah," (master's thesis, University of Utah, 1962), pp. 71, 97-99.

31. H. W Prickett, "Utah's Freight Rate Adjustment," *New West Magazine* 10 (January 1919): 44-47; "Canners Assert Rates Ruinous," *Utah Payroll Builder* 9 (March 1922): 7; *Salt Lake Tribune,* 22, 25, 29 May and 9 November 1921; Brad E. Hainsworth, "Utah State Elections, 1916-1924," (Ph.D. dissertation, University of Utah, 1968); and U.S. *Congressional Record,* 66th Congress, 2nd Session (1919), p. 647.

32. Lester T. Hansen, "An Economic Analysis of the Possible Implications of the Abolition of the Basing Point System of Pricing on the Steel Industry in Utah," (master's thesis, Utah State University, 1950), pp. 25-29.

33. *Salt Lake Tribune,* 6 April and 22 November 1921. See figures 3.8 and 3.9.

34. *Salt Lake Tribune,* 1 April and 2 July 1922.

35. *Federal Reserve Bulletin* 7 (March 1921): 273; ibid., (October 1921): 1155; *Salt Lake Tribune,* 1 January and 6 April 1921.

36. *Salt Lake Tribune,* 19 and 20 March, 30 April, 3 June, 2 and 19 July, 22 September, 21 November, and 21 December 1921, 20 October 1922.

37. Statistics compiled from the *Federal Reserve Bulletin;* Elmus R. Wicker, *Federal Reserve Monetary Policy, 1917-1933* (New York, 1966), chapters 2 and 3.

38. Stucki, *Commercial Banking in Utah,* pp. 26, 42-43, 48, 115-16; Galbraith, *The Great Crash,* pp. 184-85.

39. State of Utah, *Fourteenth Biennial Report of the State Board of Equalization and Assessment of Utah for the Years 1923-24,* pp. 5-6; ibid., *1920-22,* p. 9; *Salt Lake Tribune,* 3 September 1921. See fig. 3.10 and table 3.6.

40. *Salt Lake Tribune,* 17 February, 10 and 17 April, 7, 10, 14, 17, and 24 July, 3 and 23 August, 9 and 16 September, 11 and 30 October, and 3 November 1921, 27 January 1922. See table 3.6 and fig. 3.10.

41. *Salt Lake Tribune,* 5 and 14 January, 6, 15, 21, 25, and 28 March, 2, 7, and 14 April, 30 May, 22, 28, and 31 July, 7 and 9 October, and 25 November 1921, 15, 17, 19, 20, and 30 January, 1, 2, 7, 16, 17, 18, and 19 February, 11, 12, 16, 20, and 22 March, 9 June, and 4 August 1922.

42. Ibid., 18 January, 17 March, and 6 April 1921, 26 and 28 January and 14 and 15 February 1922.

43. Arrington, *Beet Sugar,* p. 98; James H. Shideler, *Farm Crisis, 1919-1923* (Berkeley and Los Angeles, 1957), pp. 195-96; Gwynn Barrett and Leonard J. Arrington, "The 1921 Depression: Its Impact on Idaho," *Idaho Yesterdays* 15 (September 1971): 11-12; and *Salt Lake Tribune,* 16 and 20 March, 6 and 12 April, 10 August, 12 September, 9 and 20 October, 3, 9, 15, and 20 November, 6 and 9 December 1921 and 21 May 1922.

44. Shideler, *Farm Crisis,* pp. 73-75; Barrett and Arrington, "The 1921 Depression," p. 14; 42 *Statutes at Large,* 9; ibid., 858.

45. Shideler, *Farm Crisis,* pp. 185-86; Moser, *Beet Sugar,* pp. i-ii; Barrett and Arrington, "The 1921 Depression," p. 14.

46. *Statistical Abstract of the United States, 1924,* pp. 594, 605, 647, 689; State of Utah, *Report of the State Board of Agriculture, 1923,* pp. 76-77. See, however, Barrett and Arrington, "The 1921 Depression," pp. 14-15.

47. Wicker, *Federal Reserve Policy,* pp. 37-45; Milton Friedman and Anna Jacobson Schwartz, *A Monetary History of the United States, 1867-1960* (Princeton, 1963), p. 229; and *Federal Reserve Bulletin* 5 (June 1919): 523. Statistics on the discount rate at Salt Lake City banks were cited monthly in the *Federal Reserve Bulletin.*

48. Sheelwant Bapurao Pawar, "An Environmental Study of the Development of the Utah Labor Movement, 1860-1935," (Ph.D. dissertation, University of Utah, 1968), passim; Charla Woodbury, "A Study of the Development of Nativism in Utah's Institutions, 1917-1925," (seminar paper, Brigham Young University, 1968), pp. 19, 25, 28; and Helen Zeese Papanikolas, "The Greeks of Carbon County," *Utah Historical Quarterly* 22 (April 1954): 151-64.

49. Pawar, "Utah Labor Movement," pp. 334-50.

50. Dee Scorup, "A History of Organized Labor in Utah," (master's thesis, University of Utah, 1935), pp. 28-31; Pawar, "Utah Labor Movement," pp. 351-57, 366-72; Joseph C. Clark, Jr., "A History of Strikes in Utah," (master's thesis, University of Utah, 1953), p. 11.

51. Pawar, "Utah Labor Movement," pp. 388-90, 397-98; Scorup, "Organized Labor," pp. 42-44. LDS Church leaders declined to go along with the idea of refusing to employ men who belonged to unions, however, and welcomed the passage of the Norris-LaGuardia Act. See Pawar, "Utah Labor Movement," p. 453.

52. *Federal Reserve Bulletin* 5 (March 1919): 216-17; ibid., (April 1919): 322-23; ibid., 7 (February 1921): 142; *Salt Lake Tribune*, 13 and 14 January, 25 February, 10, 11, and 20 March, 24 and 25 May, 1, 6, and 9 June, 17 and 20 August, and 1 and 18 September 1921, 24 February, 8 and 9 April, 6 May, 7 June, 8 August, 1 and 15 September, and 9 and 29 October 1922.

53. Arrington, *Economic Structure*, pp. 46-49; U.S. Bureau of the Census, *Historical Statistics of the United States, Colonial Times to 1957* (Washington, 1961), p. 45. Actually, Utah lost two hundred people between 1910 and 1920. Impressions would lead one to believe that most of this out-migration took place after World War I. Between 1920 and 1930, however, every state in the Mountain West except Arizona and Nevada lost population.

54. In fact, if land entries are any criteria, the closing of the frontier may well be dated in 1921 or 1922, after which there is a rapid drop in land entries of all types. U.S. Bureau of the Census, *Historical Statistics*, p. 237; Arrington, *Economic Structure*, pp. 35-38, 46-48. See fig. 3.5.

55. Arrington, *Beet Sugar*, pp. 101, 123.

56. Lee et al., *Population Redistribution*. 1:697; Harvey S. Perloff, Edgar S. Dunn, Jr., Eric E. Lampard, and Richard F. Muth. *Regions, Resources,*

and Economic Growth (Baltimore, 1960). p. 51; Arrington, *Economic Structure,* pp. 35-36. See fig. 3.6.

57. See fig. 3.2.

58. Idaho, for instance, showed a net increase in employment in manufacturing in 1929 over 1919. Of 15,658 employees in 1929, however, more than 11,700 were employed in manufacturing lumber. Census Bureau, *Fifteenth Census, Manufacturers, 1929,* 3:133.

59. Arrington, *Economic Structure,* pp. 62-63.

Index

This index was prepared with the assistance of Christine Miller.

Brigham
Young
University
Press